2 (8-98) 0

The Art of Talk

Art Bell

Editor: Jennifer L. Osborn

PAPER CHASE PRESS
New Orleans, Louisiana

The Art of Talk

Author and Cover Photo:
Clint Karlson

PAPER CHASE PRESS
5721 Magazine Street, Suite 152
New Orleans, Louisiana 70115

Printed in the United States

To my soulmate and wife Ramona,
who brought love into my life

CONTENTS

PREFACE

From out of the dark desert night, the music of Cusco drifts over the airwaves, your local affiliate's announcer announces the new program, and the voice of Art Bell resonates in your ears like an old friend. It is about 10:00 on a weeknight and another session of *Coast to Coast AM* has begun. Art comments on the news of the day, tells you about products from the C. Crane Company, then opens the lines to his millions of listeners, all of whom are eager to interact with this radio guru.

Who *is* Art Bell? The first time I remember listening to Art Bell was in college. I wasn't sleeping very well because of various pressures in my life, and I hit upon the idea of turning the radio on late that night for some company. I drifted away, only to be awakened later in the morning, say, 2am, by the call of Art Bell's voice. Once my mind engaged with that voice, it was impossible to go back to sleep — and I didn't want to anyway at that point. I was *compelled* to listen; I had no choice. I was gripped by the expanse of subject material covered in the show, I was fascinated by things Art talked about that I had little or no knowledge of. Art Bell quickly became a comfortable habit at night; like a good book you just can't put down, you hope it never ends.

Perhaps you have had a similar experience of initiation into the realm of Art Bell. Perhaps you, too, are inexorably linked to the Kingdom of Nye. Just like millions of other listeners, myself included, you have broadened your horizons to include the vast and beautiful Nevada desert.

I am someone who has actually met and had the honor of working with Art Bell. It was quite a surreal experience to finally meet this man, who, although fairly ordinary in appearance, holds such a captive audience. He opened the door to what he calls his "lovely double-wide" mobile home, blinking in the brightness of the desert sun. "I've just gotten up," he reveals, "Come in and sit down." He, clad in loose, baggy sleeping attire, disappeared into a bedroom to change. I, confronted now with the reality of the man behind the radio personality, feel myself blitzed with the newness of the situation. At the same time, I am comforted by the realization that Art Bell is a man who lives in a house, eats when he's hungry, sleeps when he's tired, just like us all.

You are reading this book because of — no kidding — a late night inspiration. But perhaps that is appropriate anyway. Art had just started another session of *Coast to Coast*, I think it was a Tuesday night, and I thought, God, this man is fantastic, he should do a book. Wouldn't it be interesting to read about what brought him to this point? Wouldn't it be fascinating to see what were the forces that shaped him into the person he is today? Funny thing is, Art had this in mind, too, except that he had reserved public comment on it until more than a week later. Anyway, I contacted the publisher. After a week of talking to Chancellor and receiving phone messages from Art himself, the wheels were set in motion.

Working with Art on this book was in many ways a moving experience. For probably the first time, he was reflecting upon the moments of his life, events good and bad, times trying and uplifting. Such a level of honesty came forth and such a deep sincerity of thoughts and feelings that it was impossible not to be affected. As one of his long-time listeners, to have the opportunity to talk to him on a daily basis about the unfolding of his life story instilled in me an even greater respect and liking for this man and what he represents to all his listeners.

8

The Art of Talk is more than just a life story. Art Bell is more than just a talk radio host. Because of the predominant role Art has taken in late night talk radio, this book has come into being. The trend in talk radio has overtaken America, surging in importance as we approach the turn of the century and ask for answers to more of the difficult questions that lie ahead for our world. *The Art of Talk*, then, is an extension of *Coast to Coast AM* and of *Dreamland*. It is a way to find substance below the surface of a voice that has captured the imaginations of millions of Americans. It is the means for you, as first a listener and now a reader, to bring a piece of radio person and personality into your home to stay.

But who *is* Art Bell? His voice can soothe and relax you, can implore you to see new angles on well-worn subjects, can put the fear of God into you in the middle of the night with the directions the world is going in. Now, finally, you have the chance to meet Art Bell, the man behind the voice broadcasting from Pahrump, Nevada. Now, finally you can see what goes into making of a man whose radio popularity increases exponentially each day. Now, finally you can see the person who has come into your late night world and made it a more intellectually stimulating and perhaps sometimes even humorous place. The stories and anecdotes of this man's life abound. So settle down in a cozy chair and let the voice of Art Bell once again surround you as he tells you about his life.

Jennifer L. Osborn
Editor

INTRODUCTION

Let me paint you a picture of Art Bell as a kid. I can fill you in with a lot of details. Of course, I didn't even hear of the guy until we were both middle aged men, and we have not really shared a lot about our upbringings, but I can guarantee you this much . . . his childhood went something like this:

Little Art Bell was a skinny kid with a buzz cut, growing up in a military family somewhere on the East Coast. He hadn't smoked his first cigarette yet. His main concerns in life were playing with radios, filling his stomach, and playing with radios. There were radios everywhere. By the age of 13, he was a licensed "HAM," and you could most likely any time of the day or night find little Art happily banging away Morse code, already communicating with the world.

Everywhere you looked in little Art's bedroom you found radios. You found transmitters, you found antennas, and you found boxes of hallowed treasures that some might refer to as junk, but not to Art. There were tubes. Not just any tubes, but venerable ones, like 6V6's, capacitors, resistors, old chassis that once held World War II tank radios that operated somewhere around 7 MHz, and could be coaxed to tune up on 40 meters.

I know all this because at about the same time Art was into radios up to his eyebrows, there was this other little kid called, Alan — that's yours truly writing this introduction. And as little Alan, growing up in upstate New York, I had two main concerns, one was baseball, and the other was — you guessed it — radio. I was the kid who would visit the local radio stations to tell them that I listened in to their programs on a crystal set that I built myself. I was the kid whose backyard and house were covered in wires, some of which actually performed as antennas, which was far more a matter of luck than expertise. I was the kid who lived much of the same childhood as Art Bell.

Sitting against the wall with the "let's learn our solar system wallpaper" was the ultimate triumph of mankind's achievements, the pinnacle of my very existence, the huge glowing radio that was bigger than a large doghouse. This baby had a green "magic eye" with two sides that came closer together and glowed brighter as the signal got stronger. It had at least a dozen glowing tubes that on cold winter evenings helped heat my room and a huge loudspeaker with an electromagnet in it. What a radio! What a tribute to man's technological development!

Perhaps the most important and mystical attribute to this "device of the gods" was its ability to pick up shortwave radio signals. Ah, shortwave, that strange and mysterious magic medium tuned in to mysterious exotic places all over the globe. Even the name "shortwave" exuded for me pictures of mystical, magical, invisible, secret electromagnetic rays that let you peek into secret places that only the "initiated" had access to. Night after night, I would amaze my friends by tuning into Radio Moscow, The BBC, The Voice of America, Radio Canada, The Netherlands, and every so often, Tokyo! Little did I know, off in another state in another bedroom with a different set of amazed friends, little Art Bell was tuning in to the same broadcasts.

While I was watching this big green magic eye, there was this other little kid growing up eating cereal and sending away tops for free crystal radio sets, so he could listen to the radio all night long, and in general, dedicating his life the "magic medium," too. Of course, that boy was the one and only Art Bell.

I suppose being in the radio business myself, it was only a matter of time before Art Bell and I met. By 1988, destiny was at work arranging that day when I found myself relocating to Oregon from the East Coast. Of course, one of the first things I did was scan the radio dial. I couldn't help myself. I had to check out the local products, but more importantly, I couldn't wait to catch the am skip signals from the really big stations all over the west coast. It was during this first scanning episode that I made a giant step closer to meeting Art. Fading in and out of the ether from the giant 50,000 watt KDWN in Las Vegas, I heard an interesting voice. I stopped my scanning and began listening. I was experiencing the genius of Art Bell for the very first time.

Admittedly, the earth did not stop rotating, and the mountains did not tumble into the sea, but there was a lot that I just liked about the show. It was different. I tuned in the next night. I still liked the show. After a few days, I began wondering what Art would say about this news story, and about that news story, and other events I had heard of throughout the day. I considered myself a casual listener of Art's until that fateful night when the atmosphere conspired against me: a local thunderstorm rendered KDWN non-existent. There was no Art! I tossed and turned as sleep eluded me. I scanned the radio dial, only to find retreads of some daytime offering, or some boring totally inadequate substitute for the real thing. I wanted my fix of Art. So there I was, a jaded, cynical, industry professional, sucked into being a regular listener of the Art Bell show.

Every program director lives to create talk radio addicts. We spend lots of energy trying to calculate the magic formula that draws in listeners. How did Art get me? Believe me, I was taking notes.

Many months passed before I had the opportunity to visit Las Vegas. You can be sure that I made it a point to meet the man behind the captivating voice I heard on the radio every night. Art even let me sit in and watch him do his show. Seeing him at work proved to be not only interesting, but also educational. I got to see with my own eyes, the unique way Art has created such a bond with his audience.

When Art arrived at KDWN that night, he greeted the control room operator and discussed the broadcast log. Later, Art checked the technical equipment, played a station break, bid the now off duty operator a pleasant evening and began setting up for his show.

At this time, about thirty minutes before the start of his show, Art was totally alone (except for this special night when yours truly was watching). I witnessed Art's nightly ritual of killing the lights in all the surrounding offices as well as the studio/control room lights. He even dimmed the light in the work area and hunkered down into his operating position for the next five hours.

All the hubbub of the busy workday disappeared in the tranquility of Art's studio. Below us in the casino of the Plaza Hotel, hundreds of slot machines were in full swing. Excited guests were gathered around the various gaming tables and the huge, brightly lit room crackled with excitement. Just one story above, Art was immersed in a solitude of near darkness, bouncing meters, and a galaxy of high powered broadcast equipment. He carefully spread out news clippings, magazine articles, hand written notes, etc., in an orderly chaos all around him. All you could hear was the sound of KDWN purring through the station monitor.

At about five minutes before the top of the hour, Art checked his commercial log, poured a cup of coffee from the thermos bottle he brought with him every night, and brought up the fader from the top of the hour network newscast. By the time the news closed, the telephone lines for Art's show were already packed; every line flashed. Art hit the opening theme music, introduced the show and launched straight into his monologue. I, along with thousands of others, felt then and still feel now, that the Art Bell monologue is perhaps the best encapsulation of the day's news events to be broadcast anywhere, including NPR where I was once the Director of Operations and Engineering.

The real magic of Art's show begins when Art opens the telephone lines. He has created the mood already: the lights are dim, the staff is gone and Art is totally alone with the caller. You can feel the darkness and the conversation alone becomes the light. Art and the caller. One on one. Since Art doesn't believe in screening calls, there is a freedom and intimacy on his show that I have never seen duplicated anywhere else. Most other talk show hosts don't have the ability to bond with their audience the way Art does. His broadcast comes alive, and that particular night, thousands of people all over the western third of the United States were feeling the same thing.

That fateful visit to Las Vegas when I met Art Bell proved to be another design of destiny. I knew it would only be a matter of time before Art would become a household word. The only question was when and how. Art had found the *who* part of the equation, some investors in Las Vegas *who* knew little about the business of broadcasting. To help smooth out many of the rough edges of the syndication process, Art recommended that I be hired as a consultant, since my area of expertise is in network radio.

So that's how it all got started in my rewarding and exciting adventure of broadcasting with Art Bell. Times were not easy as we sought to get Art on the air all over the country. But times were very stimulating and fun. Art Bell and I have grown to become close friends, as well as close business associates. This is something that was clearly meant to be. Likewise, this book, which makes an account of Art's life and his start in radio, and the many ways he has touched now millions of people everywhere through his radio programs, is also something that was meant to be. I am happy to play a part in Art Bell's life. I know that all readers will come to appreciate Art Bell even more, the little kid still playing with radios and the talented radio personality.

Alan Corbeth
Former President, Chancellor Broadcasting
Vice President, Premier Radio Networks

1

THE EARLY YEARS

By the time I came into the world on June 17, 1945, Franklin Roosevelt had died in office after becoming the only man in United States history to be elected to four presidential terms. At that time, US forces were also well ensconced in Okinawa after an April 1 invasion. And within a couple of months after my birth, the first atomic bombs ever would be dropped to destroy human lives at Hiroshima and Nagasaki. And of course, 1945 would see the end of World War II. It was a monumental year — the end of an era and the beginning of a new one. And I would become very much a part of this new era, part of that tumultuous generation known as the baby boomers.

My Parents

When I think about my early years of life, when I was growing up, obviously my thoughts center on my parents. I wish I could honestly say that my childhood was a happy one. I wish I could reflect on the subject with fondness. But, I cannot. My years growing up were not altogether happy years largely because of my parents. They both had such promise when they were first wed, but it quickly deteriorated after that. It's a strange phenomenon how people can become immensely drawn to each other, only to develop a loathing for each other when they unite in matrimony. It's also a very sad thing. My father was a strong, dominant personality and my mother was not much different. There was not much balance between them because they were so similar. And they fought like hell, which made life in our household, hell. I have read that the people who best survived the Holocaust were those who buried the experience deep in their unconscious minds. It was almost as though they suffered amnesia. They didn't have recurring nightmares as did so many survivors because they completely blocked those years from their minds.

The Holocaust was a "hell on earth" and, without trying to be facetious, that could be one metaphor for the way I remember my parents' marriage. They were in fact known by their friends and acquaintances as "The Battling Bells" in three states: Connecticut, New Jersey, and Pennsylvania. Unfortunately, despite the obvious disharmony, in those days, people tended to stick it out even — as in my parents' case — for more than twenty years. I think I'll start with my father.

My Father

My father is Arthur William Bell, Jr., named after his father, my grandfather, Arthur Bell. That makes me the third Arthur William Bell. The Bells also had another thing in common: they were leaders, always at the forefront of business, politics, or society, never really the type to be followers. Francis Bell, who preceded my grandfather, was one of the early founders of the community now known as Stamford, Connecticut. Francis was a pillar of the community, as the expression goes. Then there was my grandfather who served as a Councilman-at-large in Stamford. He was followed by my father who, after attending Wesleyan University and then enlisting in the US Marine Corps Reserve while still in school, went on to become an officer—another leader. Now, in my own peculiar way, I function as a sort of leader, or at the very least, I am in the unique position of influencing people. It's interesting how things work out in line with one's heritage.

My father was the person who made my life most difficult on me as I grew up. He was a stern, driven man who expected much of himself and much of me. Years later, as an adult, it dawned on me that many of the expectations — reasonable and otherwise — that my father had of me would ultimately be what forced me toward my tendencies as a driven, ambitious man.

My father grew up in a fairly well-to-do family from Stamford, Connecticut. He went to South Kent prep school and eventually gained entrance into the prestigious Wesleyan University. He was smart, studious, and always was generally serious-minded, characteristics which would remain with him all his life. While at Wesleyan, my father was no doubt affected by the fervor over the events concerning World War II. Maybe that explains his reasoning when, still an undergraduate, he enlisted in the Marines in June 1940, and was sent to Officers Candidate School in Quantico, Virginia, graduating as a second lieutenant in 1942. It did not take long before he was called to duty and his ideal of serving his country quickly became reality.

Guadalcanal

In the summer of 1942, my father was summoned by the Marines to receive officer training at the Philadelphia Navy Yard, achieving the rank of Captain after four months. Then, on June 18th, 1942, his life would change forever: he was sent into combat at Guadalcanal to command a battery of 37mm antitank guns. Later on, when he returned after miraculously having survived, he was asked by a reporter for the *Stamford Advocate* about his experience in combat versus returning home. The horrors of the war were such that many combat veterans generally believed that the rigors of combat represented reality, while home was, by contrast, a fantasy. Oddly enough, despite the intensity of his experience, my father explained, "I feel I've been dreaming the war, and I've just woken up."

What my father "dreamed" was not a pretty picture. Guadalcanal, as well as the Florida and Savo islands of that region was the object of attention at the time because of a much- coveted airstrip on Guadalcanal. Both Japanese and Allied forces viewed the island and the surrounding area as a strategic location in the South Pacific. Captain Arthur Bell's mission was to fight off the Japanese as the Allied forces made an attempt to control the airstrip. The fighting over this little airstrip was voracious. At one point during the ordeal, the Japanese had battleships with 14-inch cannons positioned at night off the shore of Guadalcanal, relentlessly pounding high explosives into the Marine holdings.

Telling of his harrowing experience, Captain Bell recalled that "when they shone their searchlights into your eyes, it seemed as though they were ten feet away. The shelling of the battleships was the most terrible of all the ordeals of Guadalcanal. You went down into your [fox]hole with a shattering feeling of helplessness and ignorance. You didn't have the slightest idea where the next shell would explode.

"You saw a blur of light in the sky, you heard an explosion as the shell left the gun's mouth and instantly you heard a rumble like a freight train overhead, followed by a terrific crack when the shell exploded."

By February, 1943, my father returned home, relieved, but still of the opinion that "the Marine Corps offered a fine career." Fate was to dictate otherwise. He would eventually end up at Camp Lejeune, the Marine base at New River, North Carolina, where he would meet my mother.

My Mother

My mother, the former Jane Lee Gumaer, was born in Washington, D.C. and raised in Essex County, New Jersey. Now, her father, my grandfather, Albert Pruden Gumaer, was also connected with the armed forces and was in a position of leadership. In his case, he graduated from the First Plattsburgh

New York training camp, and eventually became a Major in the US Army Quartermaster Corps. Later, when he was no longer in the Army, my grandfather worked in an executive capacity for McGraw Hill Publishing Company in New York City and later founded a publishing company that produced a periodical called *Textile Age*. Known to us grandchildren as "Bop," my grandfather was an ambitious, self-motivated man, and this affected my mother. My mother also feels that I have inherited many of his qualities and even look a lot like him. She insists that he was as "one track" as I am, in my case, with radio. Incidentally, leadership runs in my mother's side of the family all the way back to DeWitt Clinton, former Governor of New York.

Just as my father, my mother lived in a well-to-do environment, and had the privilege of attending good schools. My mother attended Columbia High School in New Jersey and then went to Syracuse University in New York. She eventually graduated from Coleman Business College (years later, in 1982, my mother would earn a degree from Western Connecticut University). My mother has always had an active mind, and was very ambitious, even contemplating starting her own business in those early days. And for about five years, after graduating from Coleman, she actually ran her own dance school in Maplewood, New Jersey.

Sergeant Jane

At one point during these years after graduating from school, as my mother tried to give herself some form of direction, she worked for the Alexander Hamilton Institute, and then for the American Cyanamid Company. But my mother also had a sense of duty to her country. As I indicated, her father was a veteran of rank. And she felt the patriotic inclination of the day to do her part. So, on March 15th, 1943, at Brooklyn Navy Yard, New York, my mother was sworn into the US Marine Corps Women's Reserve. By May, my mother had been initiated into boot camp at Hunter College, New York, and from there to non-commissioned officers school. Subsequently, she was assigned first to Marine Corps Headquarters in Arlington, Virginia and finally to Camp Lejeune at New River, North Carolina. This training prepared her to become one of this country's first platoon drill sergeants in the Marines. This meant she had the important task of training new female Marine recruits. She was particularly suited to this duty as she had taught dancing as a teenager and the cadence of close order drill came naturally to her. This achievement was significant enough that she received attention in several newspapers.

While at Camp Lejeune, my mom had a hand in directing a couple of war bond shows and edited a gossip column called *The Woman's Angle*. She remembers that in these early days, women marines were known by male marines as "broad-axled Marines." My mom never minded this nickname, she said, because she felt it was good-humored and based on the truth. These days, of course, that name would probably be labeled sexist. In any case, she remembers her time in the service as a great experience.

Boy Meets Girl

The fateful meeting of these two tough, disciplined, serious minded Marines took place while both were visiting their families at the Stamford Yacht Club at Shippan Point, Connecticut, a club my mother's parents had belonged to for years. It happened as many chance encounters do: boy meets girl and sees charm or beauty and falls in love. My father must have seen such a certain quality in my mother. I'll let my mother tell the story in her own words:

"My mother, your grandmother "E," suggested that the two of us have dinner at the Yacht Club. Your grandfather was out of town on business. I wasn't too enthusiastic, but decided that anything would be preferable to sitting around at home.

"We were enjoying a cocktail in the Club bar and chatting with some friends when your father walked in. I remember thinking, 'What a great looking guy!' From a distance, I guessed he was Army because his green uniform was very faded and the insignia tarnished. Then I saw the Marine emblem and, at the same moment, our eyes met and held across the room. A moment later, the waiter told us our table was ready and we went upstairs to have dinner.

"The next night, I had a phone call from your father. He had inquired about me at the Yacht Club desk. We dated that evening, and the next, and the next, and by the time I had to return to Camp Lejeune, we were in love.

"Your dad had orders to return for the West Coast, but wrote to Marine Corps headquarters and requested duty at Camp Lejeune. His request was, of course, granted.

"We continued to date on base, a somewhat hazardous proposition because your father was an officer and I a sergeant; fraternization was strictly frowned upon in those days."

After the better part of a year, my parents were engaged to be married in August 1944. In those days, the idea of marriage and weddings still held the strength of tradition and endurance. My parents were in love and, perhaps like most people then, truly believed it was forever. Both of them must have thought their stint with the Marines would be short-lived. My father seemed to imply this in a *Stamford Advocate* interview over a year earlier that quoted him as saying, "I get to thinking about a rose-covered cottage with a white picket fence and all the trimmings, and I wonder whether I was cut out to be a wandering Marine."

For my mother, her marriage to my father would mark the direction she thought she needed for her life — just as so many other women of the day. There was an idealism that pervaded the country in the Forties, particularly at the end of World War II. The majority of Americans wanted to get on with their lives, get married and have babies. My parents, quite frankly, were no different.

For the record, my parents were married at the First Presbyterian Church in Stamford, Connecticut, on a Saturday afternoon, August 26, 1944. Leading up to this momentous event were the usual array of wedding showers, parties, dinners, even a rehearsal dinner at the Woodway Beach Club. Nearly every newspaper in the area had some announcement of the wedding, complete with photos, and detailed descriptions of what my mother would and ultimately did wear to the affair.

Here's Art!

Mathematically, I do not believe I was conceived as a honeymoon baby. But I came pretty damn close, as it was only about ten months later that I emerged into this mixed up world. My mother would tell you that she knew she was pregnant because the smell of coffee from the mess hall, ordinarily something she found pleasant and fragrant made her run for cover. The night before I was born, my mother had bought my dad a pair of sunglasses as a present and stashed them under his pillow. When her water broke early the next morning, June 17, 1945 — Father's Day that year — my dad lifted her over to his side of the bed and in the excitement of the moment, the glasses were shattered into a million pieces.

The trip to the hospital was on the chaotic side, too. The MPs stopped my father for speeding on the base, but fortunately, he was able to convince them that time was of the essence. They ended up providing us with a military escort, complete with sirens, to Camp Lejeune Family Hospital. I took my first breath in this world at 12:23pm, just four days before the Japanese finally surrendered at Okinawa. I was a long baby — 22 ½ inches — and weighed in at 7 pounds, 9 ounces. Duly named Arthur William Bell, III, my mother would eventually call me Trey (pronounced "Tray"); I looked it up in the dictionary and it means "a throw or play of three at dice, dominoes or cards." The nickname stuck, although I remember taking a brief dislike to the name Arthur and, at one point, announcing to anyone who would listen that I wanted to be known as "Bill" Bell from then on.

It is always interesting to know a baby's first word, if only out of curiosity. Now, I'm skeptical of this, but my mother claims that one of my first attempts at communicating at this early age came in the form of an utterance I made that sounded like "la-dio," which she insists could only be translated to mean "ra-dio," which in effect foretold my future. I don't know. Anything is possible.

My Sisters

I am the oldest of three children: my sister, Tina, is two years younger, and Jesse is the youngest, four years apart from me. Jesse was christened Barbara Lee after my mother's sister, but legally changed her name somewhere along the line and frankly, the name Jesse seems to suit her personality better anyway. Probably ruffled my aunt's feathers a bit, though! Jesse was a tomboy in her early years, crazy about horses, fun-loving and active in sports. I can remember tickling her a lot.

Tina, on the other hand, was very serious and lady-like, even when she was a little girl. Much as I now love my sisters, however, as children, they did tend to push me out of the limelight as they made their respective appearances and that, for me, was hard to bear. As you can guess, I don't like to take a back seat to anyone. For the most part, I adapted well to other siblings, notwithstanding the usual teasing and occasional mean tricks.

One day, when my grandmother "E" was visiting, she and my mother were admiring my sister, Tina, the newest arrival in the household. The story goes that while the grownups were cooing over baby Tina, consumed with jealousy, I picked up my sterling silver, monogrammed cup and let her have it squarely on the top of her blonde head. No permanent harm resulted to Tina, but my cup bears a deep dent to this day.

I next directed my attention to my youngest sister, who came along two years later. Jess has a permanent mark on the bridge of her nose where I winged her with my sandbox shovel. In this and other incidents, I was determined to make myself the star of the family, no matter what it took.

I haven't seen much of my sisters in recent years as Jesse lives in West Hartford, Connecticut and Tina in Berkeley, California; we're all so busy with our own lives that reunions have been few and far between.

Can't Stand Still

Shortly after my birth, World War II came to a painful, grinding close. During these profound historical times, I lived my first two months of life at Camp Lejeune. I don't remember any of it. My father's association with the service ended with World War II. His inclination to constantly change civilian jobs — whether it was selling encyclopedias, peddling life insurance, or a sudden whim to go to law school — kept us moving beginning with Stamford, Connecticut, several years later to New Jersey, and from there to Media, Pennsylvania, until I was about nine. It seems the moment we started to feel somewhat comfortable in a place, we had to pick up stakes and move on. Making friends with classmates or other children was barely possible. How could you possibly nurture a friendship when in a matter of months you might never see those people again?

My earliest recollection as a child came when we were in Stamford. I was about two years old and my mother had put me down for a nap in my crib. Not really sleepy and imbued with the curiosity that can drive the mother of a two-year old crazy, I climbed out of my crib and padded over to this beautiful cedar closet of my mother's. You know how wonderfully fragrant unpainted cedar can be; naturally, I must have been drawn to it. Inside the closet, I found a paintbrush and a can of paint. Well, I started with the cedar closet and, being pleased with that effort, I continued to paint everything else: the walls, the floor, even the clothing and shoes and anything else that happened to cross my path including myself. When I had finally exhausted both myself and the can of paint, I had covered the cedar closet as far up as I could reach in this hideous shade of yellow. You can imagine how thrilled my parents were over this.

My mother fondly remembers the day, also at the age of two, that, while she was gardening, she suddenly looked up to find a circle of adults not too far from her. Suspecting as only a mother can that one of her children might be involved, she ran over to the group to find that I was standing amidst them, chattering happily and as naked as a peeled banana. Perhaps there were indeed early signs of my future interaction with the world.

The Battling Bells Take Their Toll

Probably what had the greatest impact on me during my childhood were the battles of my parents. As much as I love both my parents, it is clear that my parents were not happy with each other. As marines, they were both very much alike, but in a way that was destructive to their relationship. They were hard, driven, difficult people. The consequence of combining two people like this was constant fighting. They really tore into each other. I remember lying in bed and hearing things crashing around the house as my parents fought into the night.

And because this was not something isolated which would occur every so often, but was something ongoing and continual, many of my childhood memories are clouded. I learned much later, as an adult, that my parents were resolved to stay together only for the sake of their children. This, I believe, was a mistake, not only for them, but also for anyone who does it. My sisters and I were certainly affected by this environment. Today, I recognize what they were doing and I forgive them; they simply thought that they were doing the right thing at the time. And at the time, I believe it had an effect on many aspects of my life, including my school years.

I Hated School

If I could name the most boring thing I can remember in my life, it would be school. I began my school career when we lived in Stamford, Connecticut. Right from the very beginning, all the way through junior high and high school, I hated school. The subjects generally bored me, the teachers bored me, the whole experience was boring! I remember watching the clock that was invariably on the wall of each classroom, marking off the passage of time until I could be free to do what I wanted. Consequently, my grades were never particularly high. How can you apply yourself when you don't find anything interesting? And of course I'm sure that my home life had something to do with my inability to become interested in school.

In order to amuse myself and get through the tedium of school, I was a nuisance: to my classmates, my teachers, and everyone else who was within range. You could count on me to be the kid who always got into some trouble. I played dirty tricks on other kids, talked back to the teacher, got into arguments, and so on. I was the pain-in-the-ass who would put the tack on a seat for someone to sit down on, or fire spit wads across a classroom to pelt someone in the neck. I was the one who would rocket a rubber band at someone, challenge authority whatever way possible, make faces or disgusting noises during class, and on and on.

Of course, these actions had their consequences. I remember when I was in fifth grade I had a Latin teacher, Mrs. Brubaker, who had this rule that talking during class earned a strike from a ruler. Well, needless to say, despite numerous warnings, I would *not* shut up and the wrath of her ruler would come crashing down on my poor knuckles. I despised Mrs. Brubaker. She was a fat duck of a woman. She looked like she had inhaled two or three women, just a horrible hunk of a woman.

My parents did not know what to do with me either. I remember my father reprimanding me and telling me that I was stupid and that I would never amount to anything. Frustrated with me, he would insist, "Art, you should take school more seriously. In this day and age, a man can't amount to anything unless he gets an education."

That was the thinking of that generation. You did well in school, went to college, graduated, got a good job at a good company, got married, raised a family, and lived happily ever after. I, of course, saw no point to this and continued in my wayward ways. And although my father would attempt to discipline me, I just got all the more rambunctious.

Candy, Lima Beans & Rockets

Yes, I really was a hell-raiser. In fact, my sisters and I were all a bunch of little hell-raisers. But my parents really did try to keep us in line. They did not slack in the area of discipline. I remember when I was about six years old, I stole some candy from the store down the street. When I brought it home, my mother knew damn well that I had stolen that candy. To teach me a lesson, she marched me directly to the store and had me confess to my crime and pay for it on the spot. If I think about it, I can still recall the sick, nervous feeling I had in my stomach and the hot flush that rose quickly to my face. Obviously, this was an unbelievably embarrassing experience for me and the lesson was learned.

My mother was also unrelenting about various rules she maintained in the house. For example, we had to eat everything that was served on our plates before we could get dessert — including the most dreaded things on earth: lima beans and peas. In my opinion, lima beans and peas are the vegetables from hell. But being about as cunning as I was unruly, I devised a way to consume these horrible things. I would get a full glass of milk and put a lima bean on my tongue and swallow it like a pill.

As I got a little older, between the ages of 10 and 14, I became a little more sophisticated in my form of hell-raising. For one thing, I developed an interest in rockets, bombs, and all sorts of electrical stuff. First I learned how to build rockets. This required a few basic materials: heavy cardboard, tape and lots and lots of Ohio Blue Tip matches. I would use the heavy cardboard to construct the rocket body by making a cylinder and securing it with tape. To this, I would add the appropriate fins and a cone for the top of the rocket. Then, for fuel, I would take thousands of Ohio Blue Tip matches and remove the heads of each match.

Now these matches are extremely volatile things. They're designed so that if you strike them on some resistant surface, they ignite instantly. Well, despite this danger, I would spend hours and hours and hours removing the tips of these matches as the basis for my fuel, and then tamp them into my cardboard cylinder rocket. The tamping was extremely dangerous because the resistance between the match heads rubbing each other could set them all off. I built many rockets, and on one fateful day it happened: one of these homemade rockets blew up in my hands. Through some miracle, I remained unscathed, but the blast singed the concrete floor and the ceiling of our garage.

Then I decided to construct a metal rocket; only this time, to give it greater thrust because of the weight of the metal tube that I used for the rocket body, I included a little gasoline along with the match heads. I got an old rain gutter that was lying around the house at the time, put my rocket inside, leaned the gutter up in the crook of a tree limb in our yard, and lit the rocket. KABLAM!!! The rocket did not lift off, but instead it became a terrifying bomb, blasting apart the rain gutter into millions of pieces and ripping off the limb of the tree. Boy, what a disaster! To this day, I still marvel at the fact that I did not get hurt or killed by the shrapnel. As many times as my rockets worked just fine, lifting into the air without mishap, there were just as many incidents where I could have been seriously injured.

Despite any possible danger, one mischievous escapade led to another. I have always been fascinated by electricity: how it works, what you can do with it, etc. One day I decided to apply my fascination for electrical things to my bomb making experience. I got some cherry bombs (which are maybe ten times more powerful than the average firecracker), removed and replaced the fuse with a very thin wire, the thickness of a thread. To this, I would apply 110 Volts of electricity and FOOSHHH!, the cherry bomb would flash.

With this knowledge, I decided to rig up my backyard lawn as a minefield.

Every few feet, I buried a cherry bomb connected to a wire that led to a panel I had in my room. The panel had switches and lights, an impressive invention. My plan was to wait until my neighbor, a boy who lived next door, entered the yard so I could commence exploding one bomb after the other to get him to hop around in a comical fashion. Well, I eventually got impatient, and just started to set these things off. What a mess! In a matter of minutes, huge pieces of turf were blown into the air all over the place. I basically blew up my lawn. Well, I never liked having to mow the lawn anyway. It seemed that I would start on one end, and by the time I was through cutting the lawn at the other end, the first end needed to be cut again. So, there, that took care of that.

I also enjoyed doing mischievous things with my sisters. I remember one time I decided to use electricity for fun and came up with the idea of building an electric chair. Naturally, to make sure my electric chair worked, I needed someone to execute. My youngest sister, Jesse, was almost always game when I came up with some new amusement, and this time was no different. Jesse eagerly volunteered to sit in my electric chair. Fortunately for her, my mother discovered what I was up to at about the time I had just finished securing the appropriate wiring on my sister's wrists and ankles. I never did find out if that thing worked, although I suspect it probably would have worked just fine.

Flight Crazy

Apart from rockets and bombs, there were two things in my life that really captured my attention and my imagination for the first twelve years of my life and in many ways became my solace. From about the age of three on, I became enthralled with flying. I had and still have to this day an abiding, deep, longing desire to fly. The idea of soaring high above the earth, looking below with a perspective you can't get any other way is partly what draws me to flight. It is also the freedom one could feel, to glide and drift along with the wind like a bird. My young albeit industrious mind devised many experiments to achieve flight.

Once I took an old umbrella and climbed to the top of a red barn. I think I may have been influenced by some cartoons or something. The idea was to launch myself, umbrella in hand, from the top of the barn and fly — or at least float. Of course, by some whim, I had enough sense to jump from the barn knowing that should anything go wrong, I could land into a pile of hay below. Well, there I was with my umbrella and off the roof I went. And just for a fleeting instant, it was as though I was airborne, actually flying! But before I could relish the thought, the umbrella collapsed inside out, and I plummeted to the hay pile below. Not being satisfied with this outcome, I just assumed I needed a different umbrella. So I tried several different brands of umbrellas in my attempt to achieve flight. None of them worked. Nevertheless, I remained enthralled at the prospect of flying.

My attempts at flight did not end with a few leaps off a barn roof. Hills were also potential launching pads. As a small child, I went to visit my grandmother in Connecticut. Her nickname was 'E' because she had a hill on the way to her house and when I was two years old and strapped into a car seat, she would say "Wheee!" as we would progress down it; 'E' was my baby version of the word. Later, it was this hill from which I attempted to launch myself (again, employing the use of various umbrellas), and I always screeched 'Eeeeeeeeeeeeeeeeeeee!' all the way down. The wind gusted up the hill as I careened down it, and for a few brief moments, I actually experienced the exhilaration of flight! But then I would crash to the ground, inflicting many a bruised knee in these aeronautical attempts. Later on in my life, I would have the actual, albeit traumatic in this case, experience of flight in Alaska on a hang glider.

When I wasn't trying to leave the ground, I was avidly reading books. I loved and still love to read, whether it's fiction or non-fiction. I read everything as a child and continue to read everything to this day, even though I do have a very busy schedule.

Art Meets the Radio

By the time I was twelve, several things occurred which would forever change my life. For one thing, my grandparents (that is, 'E') in Connecticut had a huge old RCA radio as big as I was which they gathered around constantly. It was during one of my many visits there that I had my first exposure to and immediately fell in love with radio. I listened to the AM stations at the time and I marveled at hearing voices that came from miles and miles away. Radio captivated my imagination — it was both magical and mystical to me. I was excited about radio and that excitement for radio is alive in me to this day. I am so lucky to be in an occupation that involves something for which I have a great love. Apparently, this passion I would have for radio was foretold perhaps as early as two years old.

Even at this early age, I had developed an interest in electrical things. One day, I was experimenting and managed to cut a wire off of my mother's toaster. I gathered various other materials, including a shoebox in which to house my creation, and, after some tweaking, managed to construct a spark transmitter which to my delight actually made a clicking noise you could hear in the radio. It seems that even then radio was destined to be something I would always be drawn to.

HAM Radio

Once I learned about radio, listening to it was not enough; I also wanted to talk to people. That desire to interact was paired with my discovery of HAM radio. There was a man who lived down the street from us who was instrumental in my connection with radio: Paul Weiss. Mr. Weiss was a Polish physicist by profession who was in this country to help develop alternative methods of creating nuclear fission. He was also an avid and experienced HAM radio

31

operator. Mr. Weiss not only introduced me to HAM radio, but he taught me about electronics, taught me Morse code, and then helped me prepare to take the HAM radio operator's test.

My enthusiasm for HAM radio was at such a fever pitch that I remember insisting that my mother stop at every house in the neighborhood with a tall HAM antenna. I would run up to the door, knock, and often disappear into a stranger's house, while my mother waited in the car. After what must have seemed like an eternity to her, I would emerge with some piece of radio equipment under my arm! I ended up meeting many very friendly people who eagerly talked about their hobby. By this time, my parents realized that I most likely had found my niche, my calling in life. My mother was especially encouraging. I think my parents were probably relieved that I had found something to give my life some focus. The fact is, had it not been for HAM radio, there is every reason to believe that I might have entered a life of crime, drug dealing, whatever. I thank God for HAM radio.

Eventually, when the time came to take the HAM radio exam, my mother drove me all the way to Philadelphia to the FCC building to take the test. I passed the test when I was 13 and received my current call: W6OBB. To this day I am still a HAM radio operator. I truly love being able to sit down in front of a HAM radio set and talk to people all over the world. It is a vital extension of what I am doing now, and I am convinced that had it not been for HAM, I would not be doing what I'm doing today.

Travel Lust

As I spent more and more time exploring HAM radio and talking to people all over the world, I was — perhaps not surprisingly — filled with the desire to travel. In fact, I describe the feelings I had for travel as *travel lust*. I wanted to see and experience some of the places where these people lived. I suppose the unsettling atmosphere at home with my parents constantly at battle probably encouraged this lust for travel. I urgently wanted to get away from my family and to see other places.

I did run away from home several times. One time, I packed up a small sack of food and five candy bars, determined to make my way to California. Somehow I managed to hitchhike all the way to Missouri before I had eaten all my candy bars and run out of money. Exhausted and frustrated, I called my parents and they shipped me back home on a bus. Another time I ran away, I fled to my grandparents' home in Boca Raton, Florida. I believed this was a good place to run since it was one of the few places where I had had positive experiences in the past with my family during a couple of family vacations. My grandparents were sympathetic and I stayed with them for several months, even attending Seacrest high school in Boca Raton.

Living in Florida for a while had one distinct advantage: I was able to get a perspective on my relationship with my father, always rocky at best. As it turned out, all I succeeded in doing by running away to Florida was to exchange one authoritarian figure for another. I quickly discovered that my grandfather expected me to "toe the line" just as my father did. I had to keep my room spotless (a problem with me), do well in school (still a problem with me), and help with the outside chores (always a problem with me). I'd be out there in that relentless Florida sun, grubbing around in E's garden and wishing I was anywhere else. I'd pull up a weed and two more would grow in its place. In addition, and much to my surprise, I found that I was beginning to miss my family, the friends I had been able to make, and most of all, my HAM radio equipment. Accordingly, I headed for home just as (wouldn't you know it?) my father decided to change jobs again.

I was 14 when we moved to Blue Ridge Summit, Maryland, near Fort Richie, a little town nestled in the foothills of the Appalachians and straddling the Mason-Dixon Line. We moved into a huge 30-room house with five bathrooms. Eager as I was to immerse myself in radio, I had a room on the third floor, the perfect place from which to broadcast and listen. In due course, some kindly fellow HAM presented me with a huge Japanese antenna which, to my mother's horror, I climbed up on the roof to install. I spent hours in my sanctum sanctorum, gathering QSL cards (a code confirmation signifying contact between one amateur operator and another) from all over the world. The walls of my radio room were covered with QSL cards.

Although I was able to spend time doing what I loved, there was still an undercurrent of chaos in my house that prevented me from truly being at peace and forced me to consider whether I wanted to remain there as I approached my 18th birthday. As I broached the subject of enlisting in the service, my parents probably breathed a sigh of relief as they were running out of ideas on how to deal with the black sheep of the family. Since their marriage was on very thin ice at this point, they didn't need additional problems with me. Accordingly, even though I was still only 17 at the time, they signed the necessary consent form and I was officially enlisted in the Air Force and off to see the world!

2

ARMED SERVICES

There were basically two reasons why I made a decision to enter the armed services. My home life with my parents, who were drawing closer and closer to divorce (they divorced after twenty odd years of marriage), was falling apart, and my insatiable lust for travel, to get away from home, but also to explore the world.

I was 17 when I got out of high school and I instantly enlisted in the armed services. This was in 1962 and the Vietnam fiasco was in its early stages. Anyway, at that time I just decided more or less arbitrarily that the Air Force sounded like a good part of the armed services to enter. I certainly did not want to enlist in the Marines, like my parents had done years earlier. The Marines just seemed too tough for me, and I just did not want to be associated with something of which my parents had a part.

Of course, the first part of my experience with the Air Force was eight weeks of excruciating basic training, commonly referred to as boot camp. My boot camp training was at Lakland Air Force Base. God, this was an awful experience. It was both physically and mentally demanding. They put you under tremendous pressure. They called you names, they degraded you in front of everyone, and you worked out physically like you can't imagine; it was torturous and hellish. Their aim, of course, was to weed out the weak from those who would endure. I'm not sure, but I would think that basic training is no different now than it was then. And quite frankly, the approach taken to weed people out is smart. They did not want the weaklings and they should not have the weaklings. It is important to our national defense not to have these people. After all, you want the toughest people you can get to fight for our country.

I remember, each night, when I returned to my bunk in the barracks, I wondered what I had gotten myself into. I wondered how I lost my mind and joined the Air Force. It was as though when I was at home, I was in the frying pan, and now in the Air Force I was in the fire. I was almost not sure what was worse. But I stayed throughout all eight miserable weeks of it. And through some magical means, I made it to the end. Then, after all that was done, they assigned me to become a medic.

To become a medic, I was first sent to Greenville Air Force Base, in Greenville, Mississippi, and later Gunter Air Force Base in Alabama. Finally, I was sent to Amarillo Air Force Base, in Texas. It is said of Amarillo, Texas that there is nothing except barbed wire fence between Amarillo, Texas and the North Pole. And I think it's true. Amarillo is in the Texas panhandle, and when the wind blows it is very cold and bone-chilling in the winter, and very hot and dusty in the summer. In the spring, Amarillo has thunderstorms and tornadoes (it is often referred to as the tornado belt of the country). I stayed for a period of 18 months at the hospital at Amarillo Air Force Base there in Texas. This turned out to be a very eventful 18 months.

My Humorous Tumor

Being trained as a medic and engaging in medicine as I did in the armed forces was something I very much enjoyed. Of course, I was in constant close contact with doctors and I became familiar with them on a personal basis. And military doctors, I discovered, have a very perverted sense of humor (this may very well be true of all doctors, I don't know). Well, one day an unnamed woman I knew at the time found a lump under my left shoulder blade. Naturally, I panicked.

So, I went into the hospital to have one of my doctor friends look at it. He poked around and exclaimed, "Oh yes, we have something here. We'll have to do a little surgery on this and pop it out." He went on to explain that it was probably nothing more than a little fatty tumor, which could easily be dealt with. They decided, therefore, that it was not a major operation and there was no need to put me under general anesthesia. All they needed to do was to inject a couple of shots of Xylocane, a local anesthetic to numb the area.

They took me into the operating room where they had me lay down on my stomach to inject the couple shots of Xylocane and get to work. As they began to explore this thing they discovered that it was not exactly a little tumor, but something which extended into my chest cavity. Unfortunately, once they had me opened up, they could not put me under general anesthesia to continue with the operation for some mysterious medical reason or another. Their only alternative was to pump in more Xylocane, which they did. They injected thirty more shots of Xylocane into me, and believe it or not, I still felt them cutting around in there.

By this time, several doctors were working on me and this dragged on for several hours. Eventually, they clipped and snipped this damn tumor thing out of me. Well, those were the days when they did not have the facilities to test the tumor right there. They had to send a sample off to a lab elsewhere to find out if the thing was benign or malignant. If the results revealed that the tumor was malignant, this would mean I still had something to worry about. Anyway, they closed me up and I had to wait for the results.

About four days later, the doctor called me into his office for the results. I came in, sat down and stared at the doctor who looked at me with a very stern, concerned expression. Then he said:

"Art, I don't know how to tell you this, and I am sorry I have to tell you this, but you only have about six months."

37

When I heard this, I did what anyone else would do: my stomach turned inside out, my heart started to race, my face drained of all its blood, and I broke into a cold sweat. At this very moment, the doctor could not refrain any longer, and he cracked up laughing his ass off. Here was a man of rank, a captain, and he just fell on the floor laughing until I thought he would split. I guess he thought this must have been the funniest thing he had ever done in his whole life. I, on the other hand, did not share in his mirth, and sat sullenly by, eventually clasping my head in my hands and started to cry. It was about this time the ass of a doctor picked himself off the floor and finally realized that what he had done was not so damn funny.

The tumor they had removed was actually an unusually large fatty, benign tumor. I was okay. I must say, however, this was probably one of the scariest points of my life. And it may have contributed to my own sense of sick practical jokes. I remember once, many years later, I rolled a fake grenade into a radio studio to scare the hell out of its occupants.

Chasing Tornadoes

The other interesting story about my experience at Amarillo Air Force Base is the occasion when I got involved in establishing an illegal radio station on the base. But I'll save that story for the chapter on how I got my start in radio. Apart from my radio station experience, I had a buddy, Lynn Witlake, who shared in my radio experience, but was also a bad weather freak. We were both just fascinated by stormy weather (to this day, I am still very interested in stormy weather and talk about it on my radio program). It so happened, some years after his stint with the Air Force, my dear friend Lynn actually became a weatherman for a TV station in Lake Charles, Louisiana.

Anyway, we would get into an old Volkswagen and chase thunderheads, the most dangerous storms there are. And if there was a chance these thunderheads might produce a tornado, so much the better. We preferred pursuing tornadoes. Every so often we would chase thunderheads and tornadoes all the way into Oklahoma. The premise for engaging in this sort of foolishness was that we would film the bad weather and tornadoes with an 8mm movie camera to be sold to the local TV stations. But the fact is, we probably would have chased bad weather even if there was no chance to make money doing it. Lynn just loved turbulent weather and I quickly got hooked on bad weather, too. We must have chased dozens and dozens of storms. That Volkswagen was pelted with hail, lightening, torrential rains, dangerous winds, dust twisters, and on and on. How we ever lived through this, I don't know. This was just another one of those experiences where I should have been killed, but I wasn't.

Next Stop: Japan

After my 18-month stint at Amarillo, not long after our radio station was closed down, I received orders for transfer. My dreams for travel would be fulfilled by the Air Force in a big way. I was to be transferred to Kadena Air Force Base on the island of Okinawa, Japan. Okinawa is southwest of mainland Japan, and about 300 miles east of main land China. From Texas, the Air Force was basically sending me to the other side of the world. Quite frankly, I couldn't have been happier. I was given thirty days leave to prepare. So, I flew back home to Connecticut, packed my bags, said goodbye to my family, got on an airplane, and off I went to begin an adventure that has probably shaped the rest of my life.

When I got off the airplane at Kadena, I went through an amazing, intriguing, life altering experience. I was young, I was excited, and I was ready for adventure. It is amazing to think about how I was affected immediately as I entered into this new world of the Orient. All my senses were greatly stimulated. Every sight, every smell, every sound, every sense I had realized that everything I was accustomed to in America was different here in the Orient. This was not like traveling to Europe; this is was altogether different. Right away, I fell in love with the people, and the culture, and I even began to learn the language.

On the base, I did my job as a medic at the hospital there. Every spare moment I had, and any moment I could get off the base, I spent my time carousing, learning about the culture, and womanizing. This is when I developed my love for Oriental women. The experience was incredible to me, and I finally just figured a way to move off base. I so wanted to assimilate completely with these people. Off base, I lived as a Japanese person, living with a Japanese girl in a Japanese home. Like the Japanese, I slept on the floor on tatome mats, ate their food, wore their clothes, watched Japanese television, and so on. It was as though I were Japanese. The Air Force, of course, was not thrilled about me "cohabiting" with one of the locals; they felt that I had a barracks room on the base and that was where I should be. So to offset this, I hired an Okinawan to keep my barracks room clean and shine my shoes and put them in their place under the bed.

Even though I was having mostly an enjoyable time in Okinawa, Vietnam was in full swing. Tragically, there were growing numbers of American casualties because of what was going on in Vietnam. At the outset of the flow of American casualties, the injured were flown from Saigon all the way to the United States for treatment. There were no appropriate medical facilities in Vietnam to treat the injured there. Besides, it was probably too dangerous anyway. But the American press learned of this and created a stir, resulting in political pressure, which quickly stopped the flow of casualties to the US.

As an alternative, it was decided that the casualties would be flown to Clark Air Force Base located on the Philippines. Consequently, in an effort to assist doctors dealing with the influx of casualties, there were several times during my time stationed at Kadena Air Force Base, that I was temporarily transferred to a hospital at Clark Air Force Base. What I saw at the hospital at Clark Air Force Base was horrible and tragic. I will never forget it as long as I live. To this day, I have great difficulty thinking about it, let alone talking or writing about it. To consistently see people coming back with limbs missing and other parts of their bodies destroyed, making it impossible to live life normally again, was very, very difficult for me to see. But I helped to the extent that I could.

Not long after my brief stint at Clark Air Force Base, I was temporarily transferred to Da Nang in Vietnam to help out with casualties there. I was not on the front lines, but I saw the result of many of those who were. Again, what I saw was horrible, and is very difficult for me to think, talk or write about.

So, I was quite busy during my stint in Okinawa and in the Orient. Finally, my four years with the Air Force were up, and even leading up to that day, I really struggled in my mind about what to do. I had difficulty trying to decide whether or not I wanted to re-enlist with the Air Force and stay on several more years. I had absolutely fallen in love with the Orient, particularly the women, but I really pretty much had my fill with the Air Force. The armed forces are just too regimented and restricted for me. It was more in my nature to be free and unrestricted. This may seem strange because my life now is very structured and disciplined. But the vast difference between the structure of the armed forces and my own, is just that, my own structure is on my own terms, so I don't mind. I decided to get out of the Air Force.

In 1966, I was discharged from the Air Force at March Air Force Base in California. I did not regret leaving the Air Force, but I did regret leaving the Orient when I was in California. I missed it. Nonetheless, I resigned myself to my decision at the time, and decided to take some time to get my bearings. I started off by hitchhiking across the US back to my family in Connecticut. By this time, of course, my parents were divorced (they had divorced while I was in the Air Force). First, I spent some time living with my mother in New Haven, Connecticut. Then I went to live for a while with my dad in Newark, New Jersey. While I lived with my dad, I went out and got a job in the civilian sector as a technician working for International Telephone and Telegraph (ITT).

All the while I missed radio, especially after all the fun and excitement I had with the illegal radio station I helped create at Amarillo Air Force Base, and I missed the Orient. But first I decided to satisfy my hunger to work in radio, and think of a way I could return to the Orient. But again, these details are more appropriate for the chapter on how I got my start in radio.

3

WOMEN

God, how I love beautiful women. I always have. I have an abiding appreciation for the female form. There is something symmetrical, poetic, logical, aesthetically perfect, and artistic about a beautiful woman. I have observed, appreciated, and lusted after beautiful women all my life, and probably always will. Now, it may seem strange, but despite my appreciation of beautiful women, I tend to like "cute" women over the classic idea of a beautiful woman, such as Marilyn Monroe or Jane Fonda. To me, the perfect example of a cute woman is Shannon Doherty. In my opinion, Shannon Doherty has the face and body of an angel, with the temperament of a devil. I like Shannon so much that I have a black and white photo of her in my studio where I do my show.

But I suppose, above all, I have a great love and perhaps even a fetish for beautiful *Oriental* women. My love of Oriental women began with my experience of living and working in the Far East for ten years from ages 18 to 28. This was while I was on duty for the Air Force, and afterwards, when I took a radio job with a station in Okinawa. I lived in Okinawa, Japan, the Philippines, and Vietnam. And I came to appreciate the beauty of Oriental women in these parts of the world. To me they are the most striking, exotic, and the sexiest women in the world.

And how does my wife feel about all this appreciation for beautiful women on my part? I'm fortunate because my wife is well humored on the subject, and not only understands my appreciation of beautiful women but will go out of her way to point out to me a beautiful woman. I believe it is normal for one woman to appreciate the body of another woman.

Now, I don't really pay attention to the bodies of other men. There may be a difference between the way men and women think about these things; I don't know. I also don't think the love my wife and I have for each other is challenged by our mutual appreciation of beautiful women. And by the way, my wife has Asian blood and has a beautiful exotic look of her own, which I find greatly attractive. I very much love my wife, and I know she loves me. My wife is not a woman who lusts after the body of another woman. We both just happen to share in this aesthetic experience. Perhaps our mutual appreciation of female beauty is not unlike our mutual appreciation of other natural forms of beauty.

Yes, yes, I know all this emphasis on the physical beauty of women appears very sexist, and yes, perhaps I am somewhat of a chauvinist. After all, I like the traditional roles for men and women: men opening doors for women, men getting up when a woman enters a room, men giving up their chair for a woman, and so on. I also prefer women in dresses versus pants, women wearing jewelry and men not, and so on. I like the good old days when men were men, and women were women. But despite my apparent chauvinism, I adamantly believe physical beauty is not the only thing attractive about women. A woman who is intelligent, well spoken, has drive and ambition, and is not afraid to speak her mind is very attractive to me. Barbra Streisand is just such a woman. I think Streisand has attractive physical attributes, but more significantly, she also has an incredible drive for perfection. She is no doubt difficult to work with, but she is such a worker, such a perfectionist, and I find this immensely attractive. My wife is also just such a woman.

Women & Radio

So when did all this fanaticism about women get started with me? Well, it all started when I was quite young. I was 15 to be exact. And my family was living in Blue Ridge Summit, Maryland. She was 13 years old and her name was Kathy Jarrett. But unlike most kids, I was not really chasing girls, or into cars, or any of that usual adolescent stuff. Radio is mostly what occupied my attention. My mother used to always chide me: "Trey, you have a one track mind — everything is radio this or radio that." Nonetheless, although I was obsessed with radio, I took a fancy for this one pretty girl, Kathy. We became acquainted at school and she lived near us, so we had a chance to get to know each other. Eventually, when things were just right, I had the opportunity to kiss her. Kathy Jarrett was the first girl I kissed.

From that point forward, I was hooked on women. No doubt about it. Women and radio. Then the day came when Kathy's family moved to Ohio. I was crushed. I'm sure at the time I thought I would never get over it. But, of course, I did. I got over it when I met other women. And as I progressed through junior high and high school, I dated several girls, but quite frankly, none of them yielded any particularly meaningful relationship, and that was that.

When I went away from home as an Air Force medic, I became involved with many women. However, most of the relationships I had were with Oriental women, mostly because I worked and lived in the Far East as I indicated a moment ago. There was one Japanese woman with whom I became involved, and she had a very strong effect on me. She was very much interested in me and in my culture, and I was fascinated by her and her culture. To me the culture of the Orient is amazing and wonderful. Unfortunately, this woman developed some serious mental health problems that proved, after many years, to be irreversible. As much as I tried and as long as I stood by her, I finally had to admit that the relationship could not endure in light of her failing health. Sadly, I returned to the United States and she lives on in my memory, preserved in my love of the Orient and the Far East.

My First Wife

When I returned to the US, and worked as a rock and roll radio disc jockey throughout my twenties, I often had women, mostly girls really, who were groupies. They often stalked me and virtually threw themselves at me. Often, I must admit, it was difficult for me to resist the advances of these women. Bear in mind, it was the very promiscuous sixties, and the concern for AIDS and the like hardly existed.

It was not until I was 35 that I encountered a woman with whom I thought I would spend the rest of my life. For purposes of privacy, I will call her Kim Davies here. As much as I adored Oriental women, Kim is not Oriental. She is, in fact, a Midwesterner who I met when I moved from the East Coast to live in San Diego, California. This was a strange, transitional time in my life when I thought I was through with radio. I suppose I was going through a period of self re-evaluation. I began working for a cable company as an electronic technician and I met Kim while working at this job. We dated each other for about a year and then she became pregnant. It was in part because Kim was pregnant that we decided to get married. Kim and I had a son who we named Art W. Bell, IV. This may not have been the most original name, but somehow I decided to perpetuate the lineage of Art Bells in the world, and Kim did not disagree. My son is now 16 years old.

I must say my ex-wife is a good woman. She was and still is a good mother of our son. The trouble is that our relationship was — I don't know any other word but "boring." When we met, we were physically attracted to each other and seemed to get along fairly amicably. She is a nice person, no question about it, but was and just is not an interesting person. She is not a deep thinker and really did not care too much about the world around her. She was content to live comfortably in her own little world and anything beyond that simply did not matter. And although she had a good, attentive mother and didn't really have any hang-ups, she never really sought to cultivate her mind.

I guess that at the outset of our relationship I simply overlooked these facts about Kim. I probably figured that she would change. That she would develop an interest in things that were important to me. Perhaps she thought that my interest in radio did not run as deeply as it does and that I would prefer to establish a routine that allowed me to concentrate wholly upon her. Unfortunately, our relationship did not go in either direction. And the fact is, it just doesn't take long before you get tired of being in a relationship where there is no common interest, let alone passion, or real, enduring love.

One also becomes weary of someone who is not interested in what is most meaningful to you. My first wife never had any interest in my radio career, or HAM radio, or just about any other aspect of my life I considered important. This became all the more apparent when I made the decision to quit my current job to take the job at KDWN. In doing this, I took a significant drop in pay. She thought I had lost my mind. But she did not understand how bored and unhappy I was with my job as a technician for the cable company. She just wanted stability and balance. I needed challenge and excitement.

I guess the worst problem was that my former wife did not excite me intellectually. Physical stimulation is important, but I definitely need and hunger for intellectual stimulation. I require fire in my life and fire in my women. With no intellectual stimulation, I wither like a flower in the 120-degree desert sun. With Kim, I felt my soul was slowly being wounded by a lack of activity and stimulation. There was no zest for life with my first wife. We were merely partners in our finances, in rearing our child, and in a mundane day-to-day existence. Life is too short to live under such circumstances.

Ramona, My Soul Mate

In my heart, I knew I needed out. I was not going to make the same mistake my parents had made — to stay in a marriage for the sake of the children (or in our case, for the sake of my son). I know my parents thought they were doing the right thing to stay together as they raised my sisters and I. But I know we suffered immensely because they stayed together. I believe it would probably have been easier and more beneficial for all involved had they just called it quits early on so we could all get on with our lives. I saw the direction my life with Kim was going, and I knew it could not go on indefinitely, even though I knew that Art, my son, might be affected emotionally by a divorce. Then Ramona entered my life.

I met Ramona (and Ramona really *is* her name), the woman who is now my wife, while we were working at KDWN, in Las Vegas, Nevada. I had a show at the time on KDWN, and Ramona had been working at the station, starting her experience there at the board. Later on, Ramona had her own radio talk show. She was on the shift before me, and I was on the following shift starting at midnight to do my show (I will add that Ramona is a very good talk show host in her own right, although she no longer works for KDWN and no longer has her own show). As I indicated, I met Ramona while I was still married to Kim. It happened that Ramona was also married at the time. Her husband (who is now deceased) was a carpenter and did not have much ambition or interest in anything other than doing his job. So, in a sense, Ramona was plagued with a similar problem of being in a tedious relationship.

Our meeting was unavoidable; it was our destiny. We could not and should not have been prevented from meeting each other. I knew right from the beginning that we were meant to be together.

Our First Meeting

Our first meeting was something Ramona and a colleague of ours at the station, Cheryl Godfrey (another talk show host), were actually busy plotting for some time. Cheryl had previously attempted to get to know me. In fact, she had toyed with the idea of having an affair with me. But when she realized I was not that type of man, that I came across as a monogamous, dutiful husband and father, she decided to leave me alone. However, that was not enough for her. Cheryl is somewhat mischievous. Apparently, because I seemed to be the quiet, thoughtful, serious type, especially when it came to my job, I was intriguing to the women around me. Cheryl regarded me as the untouchable one in the world of radio, and she encouraged Ramona to change that — to have a fling with me.

It turns out that Ramona had been a regular listener of mine for a long time and felt that she had come to know me to some extent without ever really talking to me. And although Ramona was interested in meeting me, she was more interested in talk radio than she was in meeting Art Bell. Nonetheless, Cheryl determined that the next thing to do was to introduce the two of us, but to do that, Ramona had to hang around the studio long enough for me to arrive for my shift — around 12:30am — which she did. We met, talked briefly, and much to my amazement, she kissed me on the forehead. And then, each time she saw me in the studio, she would kiss me on the forehead. Needless to say, this got my attention, and I was immensely intrigued by this unusual woman.

A Hawaiian Gift Pack

This went on for about a week, and one day I came into work and found an interesting gift she had prepared for me sitting on the board. The gift included a bag of Ethel M chocolates, a sample bag of Hawaiian Hazelnut coffee, a package of forget-me-not seeds, and a pair of handcuffs. I love chocolate, so she got me chocolate. She's part Hawaiian, so she got me the Hawaiian coffee. She got me the forget-me-not seeds to remind me of her. And the handcuffs, well, I'll let you draw your own conclusions. That evening I went home and my wife, Kim, discovered these gift items in my briefcase. At first she thought they were for her. But I am not the kind of person who would deceive anyone, so I immediately told her that I received these gifts from Ramona. She said, "Oh, this girl has a romantic interest in you." And she was correct.

Then one day, as Ramona was leaving and I was on the phone with our station manager, Claire Reese, I looked up at Ramona just as she was about to kiss me on the forehead, as she had done before, and kissed her on the mouth. Both of us felt the immediate electricity of great attraction for each other. Meanwhile, Claire kept shouting on the phone "Art, Art, are you still there?"

Finally, I invited Ramona to be on my show. And she was on with me until four in the morning. Somehow that made it all the more clear to me that she was the one for me. I learned later that Ramona, although attracted to me, did not believe that anything more than a quick affair was possible with me. She believed that normally men with children, especially when they have a son or sons, do not leave their families. I, on the other hand, saw no alternative but to marry Ramona. I was not in the least bit interested in an affair. And I made this clear to her. We eventually got to the point where we were quite open in discussing a relationship with each other. It was when we had a secret little meeting at Cheryl Godfrey's home, one Sunday evening after Ramona's show, that my feelings were made clear. She knew I was not going to have an affair with her.

Anyway, the next day I gave her a huge box of Absolutely Fresh Flowers. She thanked me, but said that she thought it best if she went on her way. Again, I told her that I could not have an affair with her, but that I was going to make her my wife. She admitted to me later that this swept her off her feet. Shortly after this, she told Cheryl Godfrey of our discussion and my bold statement concerning marriage. Cheryl exclaimed to Ramona, "You are the first one to penetrate the ice cold facade of Art Bell!"

The Perfect Woman for Me

From this point forward, Ramona and I saw each other as often as we could. It was a magical time for both of us. Her personality captivated me. She had the fire I needed in a woman. And let me

50

tell you, Ramona is a firebrand, wild in every way you can imagine. She is argumentative, has a world-class temper, and is fiercely independent. I even encourage her to go her own way, to do as she pleases. All this was and still is marvelously stimulating to me. And yet, at the same time, I was and continue to be touched by Ramona's tenderness and her love. I cherished this connection we had made. So, I purposely prevented it from becoming sexual immediately. I enjoyed the intellectual and emotional level of intimacy Ramona and I had developed; it was unlike anything either of us had experienced. In short, I had fallen in love with Ramona.

When we did become physically intimate, it was a comical sort of circumstance. We had arranged a rendezvous in the desert, far away from everything and everyone. We had built ourselves a small campfire, and spread out a blanket on the ground. We commenced paying a great deal of attention to each other. Eventually, Ramona said, "Dear, my feet are getting hot."

"Hmm, yeah, you're right, it *is* getting hot," I exclaimed. I looked down only to discover that it was not simply the heat of our passion, but that the blanket had caught fire because it was so close to the campfire. We both jumped up, threw dirt on the fire, and tamped it out. Then we resumed our affections. Not much time passed and Ramona said, "Dear, my feet are getting hot again."

"You're kidding!" I said, alarmed.

And I looked down, and behold, the damn blanket was on fire, this time worse than the first time. We survived and put that fire out, but our love continues to burn.

My wife, Ramona, and I are soul mates. We are connected intellectually, emotionally, physically, and spiritually. We understand and compliment each other. We know how to communicate with each other. We know each other in a way that brings fullness and completion to our relationship. This is something I recognized even early on as we were developing our relationship. The love I share with Ramona is not the kind of love I had with Kim. My involvement with Ramona was not a cheap, tawdry affair. It is something that stemmed from the heart and mind, and not just a foray of lust and passion. It was clear to me when I was in love with Ramona. And at that point it was clear to me the only alternative I had was to divorce my wife of eleven years and marry Ramona.

I made the best of my marriage to Kim. If anything good was going to come of it, eleven years was plenty of time for that to happen. But nothing changed for the better during those years, and I saw no hope for change. So I divorced Kim. I left everything: most of my things, the house, a car, everything. I only took some clothes and my HAM radio equipment, and that was that. Ramona also made the same decision. She had been married to a man for 14 years. She knew that she could not continue in that relationship and also left her ex-spouse without taking anything from that past. I think that between us we shared a knife, a fork, and a paper cup.

The Great Adventure

The ink on our divorce papers was barely dry at the time we got married; that's how quickly we acted. And the day we were married we both acknowledged to each other that together we were entering what we now call *the great adventure*. And a great adventure it has been. Starting with nothing together, we scraped by on one meager paycheck week in and week out for a long time. But we loved each other and we knew that was the most important thing. You can have all the material possessions in the world, but if you have no one to share it with, it means nothing. Besides, we trusted that everything else we needed would fall into place — and it has.

I know that many of my listeners will be disturbed by what I have revealed here. Most people who listen to me probably regard me as an economic and political conservative with high moral standards. Which I am and which I have. I believe divorce is a big problem in our country. I also believe people are too quick to divorce. But remaining indefinitely in a marriage devoid of love is like not living at all. As for my own experience, I have no regrets. My life is my own. And I believe my Maker is aware of all that I have done and I even doubt I have much explaining to do when I come before His presence. For I believe it was all meant to be. Not that our lives are entirely predestined for us, but I definitely believe that fate brought Ramona and I together. I know I made the right decision and the years we have had together have proven this to me. With each passing year, we have grown closer and our relationship has gotten better.

Not to be with this woman as I have would have been a sort of sin. To stay in a marriage without any love would also have been a sin. I know I would have regretted it. I am truly happy with my marriage to Ramona and I firmly believe my relationship with her has definitely contributed to my success in radio. I could not be the open and honest person I am on the air without the influence of my wife. And my openness to reveal these facts here is only possible again because of my wife's influence.

4

MY PUBLIC & PRIVATE SIDES

There is a huge difference between my professional or public life and my private life. Of course, there are areas where my professional life does tend to merge with my private life. For one thing, I am basically the same person in private as I am on the air. It would be impossible for me to do a show five hours every night without being honest. If I were not truthful, my listeners would know it. I am just myself on the air and evidently my listeners appreciate that fact. But there are a number of things about me that may or may not be especially apparent unless you get to know me personally.

Personality Traits

To begin with, I am an immensely driven, competitive person. Some may say I am egocentric. I'm not sure. If having an ego means you recognize certain innate talents in yourself, and if it means you have unrelenting drive which yields success, well, then I'm guilty; I have an ego. For I know I am good at what I do as a radio talk show host. At times, I believe I am as good at this profession as anyone in the business, whether it's Larry King or Rush Limbaugh or G. Gordon Liddy, or anyone. Is that my ego talking? Probably. But then, I'm not worried about it. My ego is very much a part of who I am.

As I said, I am driven. Some will argue that drive is genetic, but I believe my drive stems from the environment in which I grew up. On one hand, my mother was extremely nurturing, encouraging me with radio from the very beginning and supporting me in a firm but loving way in all my endeavors. In contrast, my father would tell me I was stupid, and for all the times he would insist that unless I went to college I would amount to nothing, I felt compelled to be the opposite. I needed to demonstrate that I was intelligent and that I would amount to something — my own way.

Yes, once in a while, when I did not do very well at school, I felt as though I were nothing, that perhaps I would amount to nothing. I almost believed my father. Yet, in time, this sort of discouragement on my dad's part had a strange way of inculcating the notion that I must be the best at all I do. I became very goal oriented and very competitive. I do not encourage this as a means for people to raise their children. I think it is far more useful for most people to be encouraged, and to be instilled with a sense of responsibility and discipline in order to achieve things in life.

I am extremely competitive. As you know, my career in radio is one of the most important parts of my life. So I am keenly concerned about where I am in this odd business up to the very minute. I am the first person to find out as soon as I can what my ratings are, or how many affiliates I am adding to my syndicated radio program, or how I am received in, say, Mobile, Alabama versus San Diego, California. I want to know! I need to know! I need to know that my show is good and that it is being well received. Now, some people may think my ego is gratified only when listeners express their adoration of me and of my show.

When I first started out in this business, it was very gratifying to have people compliment me on my show; this *is* important to me. But the compliments are not as important to me as the tangible results. It is critical for me to know that I am popular everywhere and that my program is becoming one of the most significant programs in the country. I will accept nothing less. Does this mean I am egocentric? Probably, but again, that is the way I am.

Goal Setting

I am a goal setter. I set goals for myself, whether they are financial, career, personal, whatever. Then I set about achieving those goals doggedly, relentlessly, not letting anything stand in my way. This does not mean that I will do anything to deliberately hurt anyone or anything that was illegal. But I will worry, and fret, and work, and think, and put up with all sorts of foolishness to achieve my goal. And when I do it, I want to be the very best at achieving those goals. I want to outperform everyone else; I want to be in first place. This quite naturally only adds to my competitiveness. And let me tell you, when things are not going my way, I can get very angry, frustrated, disappointed, and very depressed. But I won't stop there. I will try to figure out what is going wrong and to find a solution. In doing so, I often will intellectually chew things to death.

It is a sad thing when I think that just two or three decades ago, America used to set goals. When John F. Kennedy was in office, as a nation we were committed to land on the moon in a decade. And, by God, we did it. We did it in a way no one else in the world could do it. But somehow, over the years (and not many years at that, I'll add), our country has become lackadaisical, cynical, and indifferent. This country has quickly slipped into a state of mediocrity. People seem to live only day to day. They no longer care about goals. We have become soft as a nation. In my opinion, we are no longer number one in all we do in this country.

I even see the acceptance of mediocrity taught in our schools. The liberals call it outcome-based education. This means you do what you can in any given field and whatever it is you can do is just okay. Well, I believe that mediocrity is mediocrity. First place is first place, and second place is second place, and third place is third place, and so on; that is the reality. Anything else is just bullshit. As far as I'm concerned, there is only one place to be, and that's first place. This is what children should be taught. I strongly believe that, although it may seem extreme and maybe even dogmatic, a standard must be set. I even set standards in the things I buy or the things I sell on my radio program. When I go to buy a car, I buy the best I can, if it's a kitchen appliance, I try to get the best, if I want a new computer, I want the biggest, the fastest, and the best, and so on.

The Best & My Advertisers

My attitude about always having the best and being the best probably drives my broadcasting company and even my wife nuts sometimes. I have turned away many, many potential sponsors because I was not persuaded that their products were the best for my listeners. In fact, if I do not personally use and like a particular product, it does not receive advertising on my program. Believe me, I have tried dozens of vitamin products, many of which tasted like absolute garbage. Then there were the many skin care products. I remember one time I put on this face cream and my face swelled up like a basketball. I have also been approached by many people with ideas for various 900 numbers. I turned them all down.

Obviously, sooner or later I have to accept someone to advertise their products. For example, I remember when I was approached by the man who runs Absolutely Fresh Flowers (he ships fresh miniature carnations from his flower farm directly to the customer; no middle man), and he sent me a box which he claimed represented a typical shipment. I was impressed by the shipment, but I did not believe he would ship the same quantity if he didn't know I ordered them. So, I ordered the flowers under an assumed name and had them shipped to a different address. He proved himself to be consistent in quality and quantity and, as a result, instantly became a new sponsor on the program. The best is absolutely important to me, no doubt about it.

My Strong Personality

I suppose I can attribute my attitude and my drive, and all these various character traits I have described, to a very strong personality. I really *am* a strong personality and it is not unusual for me to dominate other people. I'm capable of operating like a freight train in the way I dominate other people. This is one more reason I know that my wife is good for me; she won't allow me to dominate all the time. She stands up to me. She has a great deal of strength all on her own. I love it. I admire her for it.

Despite my upbringing, which one could easily argue could have created all sorts of problems from the standpoint of my self-image, I have a great deal of self-confidence. Other people badgered by a strong father as they were growing up may have become reserved and lacking the confidence to do much of anything in life. But I actually became strong. Besides, I believe I quickly learned what I was capable of, and what my abilities were, and I learned to feel confident in them, no matter what my father did or didn't do.

Being a strong personality has also made me into a perfectionist and a control freak. When I decide to do something, I insist that it be done my way. No exceptions. And if there are other people involved with what I'm doing, they must conform to my direction. And I won't back down because I'm very stubborn. This is one reason I admire Barbra Streisand. I don't happen to agree with her political views, and I know that she is often quite difficult to work with, but she is driven, and a perfectionist, and a control freak just as I am. But then, look at all she has achieved in life.

High Strung & On Time

I suppose the same thinking which dictates my tendency to be controlling and a perfectionist is the thinking which makes me compulsive about keeping time, for appointments or for getting things done by a certain time. I abhor people who do not do this. I am either right on time or I am early. I actually pride myself on this fact. I'm a very busy person, and if I can do it, so can everyone else. If I have a meeting with someone and they are late, I get annoyed, I can't stand waiting, and I'll even get angry. Again, I am sure my compulsive behavior is probably just consistent with my desire to be the best. I always strive for excellence, for perfection, and I get disgusted so many times when all I see are people who settle for mediocrity.

I suppose one drawback about the way I am is that it may ultimately kill me. In fact, it would not surprise me if I were to die of high blood pressure or a stroke because I'm so driven, and so intense, and so manic about doing things the way I do. Besides that, I smoke.

My Desert Hideaway

I live in the middle of the desert. Pahrump, Nevada is about 65 miles west of Las Vegas. The Southern Paiutes, who occupied the Pahrump Valley centuries ago, named it "Pah," meaning water, and "Rimpi," meaning stone or rock; it developed into Pahrump, a translation of flowing waters emerging from rock. Of course, in relation to this, it is interesting to note that Pahrump does in fact sit on the third largest aquifer in the United States.

Pahrump has maybe 12,000 inhabitants, and is pretty much the last piece of civilization there is before you get to Death Valley, one of the hottest, most desolate places on earth. I am often asked, "Art, why do you live in the middle of the desert when you can live anywhere you want, doing what you do?" And my answer is always the same: "I love the desert." There are a variety of reasons I live in the desert, but the main reason is that I relish the privacy I can have. I can walk outside of my home and hear absolutely nothing. I like to stand outside and look around in nearly any direction and see absolutely nothing. This is good for me. Living in the middle of nowhere massages my soul; that is the best way I know how to describe the feeling I get. It balances me and it enables me to do what I do best every night as a radio talk show host.

I am not an ecology freak. But I love the desert so much that I utterly abhor those who seek to defile it by littering it. Evidently, there are people who look at the desert and just think it is a wasteland and is worth nothing more than to dump their garbage in it. There is nothing more horrible to me than seeing beer cans, used condoms, old mattresses, abandoned cars, tires, and on and on. I get so aggravated at this that sometimes I'll go out and pick up trash out of the desert. I just hate to see it.

Pahrump is definitely a small town. It has one traffic light and one major supermarket. And yet, this town is growing faster than I would have it. I could live anywhere. Yet, even if I were offered ten times more than what I make now, I would not relocate to any of the big cities where most of my successful peers now reside. I would never, ever live in Los Angeles, New York, or Washington D.C., or anywhere other than where I now am. In fact, I am so adamant about this that if I can do it, if I can arrange it, I will die right where I am. This is how serious I am about living in the desert, and about living here where I am right now.

My show is often hectic, tense and at times actually induces panic attacks. So, when I'm not on the air, I like privacy and I like being alone with my wife. We take long walks in the desert. People sometimes look at the desert and exclaim, "My God, what a vast wasteland you're living in, Art." Well, I'm not in a wasteland. The desert is very much alive. Just take a short walk and this will convince you quickly that the desert is vibrant with life. There are all manner of crawling, scurrying, and hopping creatures living in the desert. Most people are accustomed to living in areas where the view of the horizon is blocked by buildings or foliage. I grew up on the east coast, and I have lived in many different cities in this country and abroad, and I know what it is like to live encumbered by things all around. That may be fine for some, but not for me. I know what living in an area with trees is like, or where you can see the ocean. But to me, there is nothing that surpasses the beauty and the serenity of the desert. I love it and I will always live in the desert.

Recluse?

There are people who try to visit me in my little town of Pahrump. They will go to the local post office, or the fire department, or sometimes even the Pahrump Chamber of Commerce. No one will tell them where I live and I'm glad. There is a lady who works at the local Chamber of Commerce and she has not only told people that she doesn't disclose my whereabouts, but she also has informed them that I am a recluse. I remember one time my wife and I decided to visit this lady at the Chamber of Commerce. I went into the office and walked right up to her desk and said, "I am not a recluse!"

The lady was startled and somewhat confused by this announcement. So I repeated myself. All the while my wife was laughing hysterically as I did this.

"I am not a recluse!" I insisted.

"What do you mean?" the lady wanted to know.

"I'm Art Bell, and I'm not a recluse."

"Oh, Art Bell," she said now knowing what was going on. "Well, Mr. Bell, you don't want people to bother you, do you?"

"No," I said quietly.

"Well, I just tell people that you're a recluse and that we don't let people know where you live."

"You're right, I don't want people to visit me," I returned. "But I'm still *not* a recluse."

Apart from the attractive geographic location of the desert, I find that although I enjoy interacting with people the way I do, I don't like the close proximity of people. The open expanse of the desert affords me the privacy I need. I spend at least five hours every day communicating with many, many people. But I don't really want to be with people in person. People tend to disturb my peace and my peace of mind; they disturb my thoughts, they disturb my work. Maybe this is just the simple truth, and is a disease that may very well be sweeping the country: people are becoming less tolerant of each other. Perhaps it's because there are just too many

61

of us, and there is not enough room for all of us in most of the places we call home.

I find myself less and less tolerant of the quirks and bad habits of people, or I just find them offensive in some way. I find that I am very protective of my privacy because I enjoy all the time I have to myself and with my wife, time which is generally not shared with others. I love what I do publicly and I love what I do privately. And I want to keep these two parts of my life separate. So, the only way I can think of doing this is to have control over my privacy. If people knew where I lived, I fear they would constantly be showing up at my doorstep and this unnerves me. And as my program gains popularity, I grow ever concerned with maintaining my privacy. I don't want to become a local tourist attraction.

Does this make me a recluse? Perhaps it does. So, I guess I'll grudgingly accept that label. There you have it: Art Bell is a recluse, if this is what it means to remain private. Of course, now that I have made it clear, I suppose this will compel some people to try even harder to locate me. I sure hope not.

Home Life

I have made it no secret that I do not live in a huge mansion on an estate with a swimming pool and barbed wire fencing with guard dogs protecting my property. I'm very much in the open, and in a sense somewhat vulnerable to unexpected visits by strangers. I live in a very nice doublewide portable home, but I do not live in a trailer park per se. I am secluded for the most part, though I have a handful of neighbors nearby. I don't bug them, and they generally don't bug me. Outside of my home, of course, I have the satellite dishes that are my link to the world. My house has a tidy, unassuming appearance, and that's just how I like it. I have a couple of trees and on occasion I have tried to grow flowers and such. But I'm in the desert, so growing much of anything is a challenge. I don't have a lawn because you normally don't have lawns on a terrain that is mostly sand.

Recently I have added several elements and as a result, my home area is beginning to resemble something like Barbra Streisand's compound in Malibu, California. Mine now consists of a hot tub enclosed in its own little room. This hot tub is especially great because I don't have to put nasty chemicals like chlorine into it; instead it is ozone-cleaned. I like that technological advance! I also added a large building that no one knows what to make of until they walk through the commercial-looking, double-door entrance: a racquetball court. Built of beautiful hardwoods and professionally painted and air-conditioned, this is my newest attempt at recreation and exercise. Besides, I always wanted a court that I could use in private and now I have one!

On the inside of my home, I have a couple of bedrooms, one of which serves as my studio. The layout of the house is open and comfortable. There is an entryway where I have a pool table, there is a nice kitchen and dining area, and I have a comfortable living room with an L-shaped couch situated in front of a large screen TV which has CNN on perpetually. My house is a modest place to live, but I love it just the same. It really is all that my wife and I and our three cats need. Our home is air conditioned and filtered to keep the house clean and allergy free (my wife has allergies), and the water is filtered with magnetic technology to keep the white scaling of water stone off the pipes.

Because of our location, the place is absolutely quiet. No barking, yelping dogs or children nearby, no street traffic of any kind, really none of the usual city noise most people have to tolerate. As I said earlier, I love the serenity this place affords. It helps me think, it makes it easier to do my job, and it gives me peace of mind.

My Orderly Life

Now, being a perfectionist and very detail oriented, I must say I do have one domestic tendency that nearly drives my wife nuts: I am a neat freak. It is an affliction, and it may very well be a compulsive disorder, I don't know. But it is true; I am a neat freak.

Everything has its place and to me everything must be in its place. And I will go around the house to make sure everything is where it belongs. Then I'll go around and straighten photographs or anything else that is out of position. I can't stand things that are not symmetrical. And I will go around doing this throughout the day, just to make sure nothing has moved. I have San Tropez telephones in various strategic locations throughout the house. I have the world's best fax machine stationed in the dining area. Ashtrays have their proper locations. Audio or video tapes, various types of electronic equipment, clipboards, etc., etc., must all be in their proper place.

I believe I am this way because in order for me to do what I do for my radio program, everything around me must be in order. I need to have my life regimented: orderliness around the house, peace and quiet, I sleep at a certain time, I get up at a certain time, I do my homework (preparation for the show) at a certain time, and my show runs at a certain time (not a minute before or later). In essence, my life is ruled by the clock. But this is apparently fairly common among people such as myself who are driven, disciplined, and ambitious.

I cannot stand things that do not work. I am a compulsive Mr. Fix-it. If something does not work, I am driven to find out why it does not work and then to make it work. As a result, I have completely taken apart many things, only sometimes putting them back together again properly, and more often having to gather up the pieces lying around me and throw the whole thing in the trash. Nevertheless, I cannot bear the sight of something that does not work, and I cannot leave it alone until I have found a way to make it work.

Thus, the picture of Art Bell at home is a serene, quiet one. I fix what I can when I can, I keep the world around me in order, and I enjoy the peaceful nature of living in the desert.

Animals

I love animals. I am not an animal activist, or a "tree hugger." I'm not going to get all excited about saving, say, a certain species of rat, or chain myself to a tree to keep trees from being cut down. I just love animals. And I don't kill animals. I remember when I was a young boy, my father got me a BB gun. I became very proficient with that gun. I could split a daisy in half at fifty feet away. Later on, my dad got me a .22 rifle and I was a good shot with this, too.

One day, I saw a squirrel in a tree about 100 feet away from my upstairs bedroom. So, feeling challenged by this, I took aim and shot it. I saw the squirrel fall, and I went outside and watched that squirrel die; I cried. From that day onward, I vowed to never hunt and kill another animal ever again. I don't like the idea of people hunting animals for sport. It is one thing if you have to hunt for survival, and I would do that if necessary, but it is quite another thing to hunt just for the pleasure of killing something. That I don't do, nor do I endorse that type of activity. Some people may argue and say, "Art, don't you eat meat?" I do. "Then, aren't you hypocritical?" Perhaps. But at least I am not the one doing the killing. I just could not do it. By the way, I own guns, but only to own them and to occasionally shoot at non-living targets.

Abby, Ghost & Shadow

Each person has an animal that they love in particular, ones they keep as pets. I am a cat person and so is my wife. As my wife and I were about to commence our great adventure together, it seems fate had determined that we were to begin this experience with the company of a feline friend.

Ramona and I were married on the Las Vegas strip. It was Saturday, August 4, 1990, at about 1:15 on a hot summer morning and I had just gotten off the air from doing my radio program there at KDWN. Ramona's parents came out to Las Vegas and we had a beautiful wedding at a chapel on the strip. If you have ever been on the Las Vegas strip, you will know that it is not much different than a very busy highway, with a great deal of traffic around the clock. The chances of a little kitten surviving are slim to none at all, at best. Nonetheless, this little black waif of a kitten, scraggly fur sticking everywhere, appeared just as we were having our wedding ceremony. Someone opened the door and in it walked. As far as I'm concerned, it was a miracle. I knew immediately that that cat was our cat. When I saw it, I declared: "That's our cat!" I snatched it up and promptly took it to the car. It fell asleep right away, probably exhausted from dodging cars for who knows how long and grateful for a safe haven.

After the wedding, we went home for the reception. The reception fare included roast beef, among other delicacies. So I fixed a plate of roast beef for myself. While we were distracted with the excitement of the wedding and all, the kitten helped itself to the entire plate of roast beef and again fell asleep. We eventually named our cat, Abby Chapel, 'Abby' for the name of the Justice of the Peace who married us, and 'Chapel' for obvious reasons.

Abby started off skinny and was practically starving to death when he first came into our lives. But the moment he had a taste of that roast beef, he developed an insatiable hunger for beef products of all types, including hamburgers, meatloaf, ribs, and, of course, more roast beef. Before long, skinny Abby became Abby the fat, 22-pound cat. We have perverted this poor animal and he will eat virtually nothing but beef; he shuns fish of any kind.

Abby has only been in our company and has selfishly had us all to himself. He demands and gets attention whenever he wants it. Sometimes, when I'm already on the air, Abby will hurl his big body against the studio door to attempt to get in. This is why, on occasion, listeners may hear a thudding or thumping noise in the background. Well, that's almost certainly Abby trying to burst in and jump on my lap. One time he actually got in and jumped on my lap. And I thought, oh well, what the heck, I'll let him stay. So I turned up my microphone volume and put the microphone to

Abby who was content and purring. My listeners could clearly hear Abby purr over the air. Abby is quite a character.

My cat story does not end here. One day Abby was behaving rather oddly. He started running around the house, going into closets, going into every nook and cranny, and just running around like a nut. Ramona and I knew something was up. Sometime later, while preparing a barbecue out at the back porch, we heard a faint mewing sound come from under the house. I have a portable house that has cinder blocks for its foundation. And each cinder block has several small holes to permit ventilation beneath the house. Apparently, we had a kitten under the house, hiding behind one of these cinder blocks. The kitten evidently gained access under the house through one of these cinder block holes.

We called to it, "kitty, kitty, kitty," but it would not come out, only answering pitifully, "meow, meow." We then tried by all means to get the kitten out from under the house, including attempting to lure it with various meats, fish, and smoked Port Chatham tuna. If we left the food out, we discovered that it would be gone overnight when we could not see it. The little thing crawled out from hiding, ate and disappeared. I feared at one point that if it would continue to live this way, it would eventually get so fat, it would get stuck behind the cinder blocks and never come out. I thought what a pathetic, sad life this little animal was living. On the other hand, it was lucky to have found our place to live because otherwise the poor little thing would most likely have become coyote meat.

It's just a simple fact that in the desert cats are coyote meat. Or a cat could be carried away by one of the giant birds we have out here in the desert. Or one of the poor creatures would be flattened by a car. I just don't believe in outside cats, especially in the desert. After nearly two weeks of trying to get the cat out, it became more and more imperative that I capture the little thing for her own good. That was the next part of this odyssey: to devise a means of catching the little stray under our house.

Being fairly mechanically minded, I devised a trap. I got a large plastic US mail bin (this is how I receive my mail: by the bin full), and held up one end with a small metal rod, to which I attached a wire. As bait, I put a bowl of Science Diet cat food under the trap. I then brought the wire in through a window so I could sit and watch the trap and wait — and wait, and wait, and wait. The idea was that the kitten would go into the trap to get food, and the moment it did, I would pull the wire, thus removing the metal rod, and down the mail bin would fall, trapping the kitten inside. I sat and waited, and I did this for two days, being alert and prepared to capture the little thing.

By now I had named the kitten "Ghost" because you could never see it. Finally, I saw Ghost come out to get the food. You see, I no longer left the food out at night, so this would make the food more of an enticement. And Ghost went into the trap, all the way into the back. I pulled the wire, the metal rod came out, and down dropped the bin to catch the cat. Only, the bin dropped on Ghost's tail, leaving just enough of a space for the cat to back out and escape back into the cinder block hole under our house. I was going crazy, getting frustrated and even more determined to catch this little cat. I put on protective clothing, a pair of gloves, and took a flashlight with me. I then went beneath the house, gaining entry by removing a board intended in the first place to keep little creatures out from under the house, and pursued the kitten under the house.

After much effort, crawling around under the house, bumping my head several times on things, becoming entangled with spider webs, I was eventually stopped in my tracks by a supporting cross beam that ran the length of the house. Yet there, within view, but at the other end of the house that was inaccessible to me, Ghost was curled up watching me. I thought I would lose my mind. I backed out from under the house and was absolutely frantic.

Each night, on my radio program I gave an update, mostly out of sheer frustration, and possibly with the hope that someone might offer a solution. This went on for several more days, and I eventually received a call from a listener, a lady who worked for the Los Angeles SPCA (the animal control department) who had my solution. She sent me a special cat trap called a Have-A-Heart trap. This is an ingenious trap made of metal mesh, and the cat walks into the trap, and when the cat steps on a metal plate, the trap shuts automatically.

I set the Have-A-Heart trap and waited — for two days. I first used Science Diet as bait, and finally smoked Port Chatham tuna, which did the trick. Much to my delight, surprise, and relief, Ghost got trapped. We took Ghost and brought her into the house and put her into the bathroom with food, water, and newspapers. The next day we took Ghost to the vet for a checkup and shots, etc. Then we received a call from the vet who told us that Ghost was dying from feline leukemia, a fatal cat disease, for which there is no cure. She would die quickly and in great pain. We were also told that Ghost had an injury to her hip, which the vet assumed was the result of the kitten being thrown from a moving car.

I was devastated. I cried. So did my wife. We felt so sorry for little Ghost. As an act of mercy, we had the vet put Ghost down. That night, I called Alan Corbeth, president of the broadcasting company, and explained to him what had happened. I told him that I didn't think I could go on the air that evening. Being a cat man, he was sympathetic and simply said, "Art, you do what you feel is best for you." After getting off the phone, I gave it some thought and decided that I would go to the local animal shelter to look at cats. My wife joined me, and we ended up spending most of the afternoon at the animal shelter looking at dozens of cats. What we noticed was that there was hardly any space for all the cats. The people who ran the shelter did as good a job as possible, they loved the animals, everything was clean and the animals were well cared for, but there just was not enough room. We also found another kitten, who we would learn was healthy, and who we named Shadow, the shadow of Ghost, because Shadow followed Ghost. Shadow is now part of our family.

That night, I went on the air anyway, although I did so with a heavy heart. I mourned Ghost's passing. But I decided to tell my listeners the story, and said, "please, if you have a couple of bucks you can rub together, send them to the Pahrump Valley Animal Shelter. And please don't tell them I requested you to do this."

Much to the surprise of the animal shelter people, and to myself, the money came pouring in; they raised more than $8,000. The lady who ran the shelter found out that I had encouraged people to do this. She contacted me and I told her the story of Ghost. With the money my listeners had raised, they planned to erect a new cat shelter, which they would name in honor of Ghost.

Abby and Shadow get along very well, although it is funny to see that little Shadow is very domineering, and tends to boss Abby around. It is good to know that I have brought Shadow into a better life. For my wife and I, that poor little pathetic waif of a kitten, Ghost, will linger in our memories forever. I have to put the whole thing into perspective in this way: at least we found Ghost and she didn't die miserably and, ironically enough, her life has amounted to good for other cats in the future.

Comet

Ghost was the first cat that was under our house. So it is my view that Comet came to us because of that. After Ghost died, we went to the animal shelter and we got Shadow. But then along comes Comet, another cat under the house.

Except this time, because of Ghost, we had the Have-A-Heart trap in advance. Anyway, about 3:30 in the morning, sure as hell, we heard, 'snap' and there was this little emaciated ball of orange fur. Comet had a great big head and not much of a body. And Comet was very, very wild. So we took him to the vet and we said do it all: claws, balls, shots, give him a bath, but before you do all that, test for feline leukemia.

Comet tested negative for feline leukemia. So we took Comet home, still in the cage, and put him in the cat bed—we have cat beds—and Ramona and I both sat there and waited, looking at

Comet, waiting, waiting. Comet finally opened his eyes, blinked a few times and went five and a half feet straight up in the air. Then he started running into walls until he got himself all bloody. I couldn't take it so I picked Comet up and he was okay, he was purring when I held him close to me. But it was not a purr of happiness; it was a purr of fright. Nevertheless, he still let me hold him (of course, he was still drugged).

So we set up a little area in the bathroom with food and water and the cat box. A day passed and I went in to Comet's area. Since I had held Comet once, I figured it would be okay and I went to pick him up again. Bad idea. Comet turned around and nailed my hand, bit me to the bone, and reflexively I let go of Comet. Then like an idiot, bleeding, I reached down to pick Comet up again and it's like I hadn't got the message, and he nailed me again. Same hand, right down to the bone. This time I got the message so I left Comet alone and I went out and nursed my hand with hydrogen peroxide. I thought I was going to be fine without stitches. Within two or three days, my hand was completely swollen like a basketball. So I had to go to the doctor and get a tetanus shot and antibiotics, etc.

Comet lived in the bathroom for the next four months. I used to suit up—I'd get into this big heavy jacket, put on gloves, and I would go in there and try to get close to Comet and touch him. He would let me do it, but not without a warning: rrrrr. He could jump vertically six feet. Finally one day he did that, clearing the barrier between the bathroom and the bedroom. He immediately decided that his new home was going to be in the chest of drawers. He found a way to get under and then he crawled up into the drawer and made himself a little nest in our underwear. And that's where Comet lived for the next three months. We didn't see much of him; he would only come out when we would go to sleep or we would be quiet. Then he would slink out, use the box or eat.

As Comet continued to eat, he got too fat to fit under the chest of drawers anymore; that is when he discovered you can live under a waterbed. For the next year, he lived under the waterbed and would come out more and more. Two years later, he is now the gentlest cat I have ever met. He intentionally withdraws his claws when he jumps so he won't scratch you. He doesn't like to sit on your lap, but he loves to be held to your chest. And he purrs and loves to be petted. Every day he does something new that brings him away from being wild and toward being domesticated. I could write a book about this; the time I have spent with him has been astounding, but it has paid off. He really loves me; now I am like his parent.

He still will not interact at all with strangers. When we had someone house sitting for us for two weeks, after 2 weeks, he would finally come out and sort of look warily at the people who were house sitting. I think and I can't know this for sure, but I think he is always going to be a two-person cat: Ramona and I. I can only imagine what his life must have been before us. He never saw a human obviously; he must have been born in the wild.

As in any situation that involves more than one animal, or human for that matter, there is a dominant cat in our household, although you would be surprised to find out that it is not sixteen-pound Comet or twenty-pound Abby. Little Shadow has them both wrapped around her paw and no one screws with her. I can't understand it, but she throws them around in a different way than with just weight.

The Rabbit Saga

I have developed a strong dislike for rabbits, although I generally like all animals. But here is how I learned to dislike rabbits.

Now I have some acreage where I live. And I have had some success, not without challenge, in growing some trees, and bushes, and a small garden on my property. In the desert, the only practical way to get water to my trees and bushes and my small garden is by irrigating all this stuff with what is called a drip system. The system is comprised of a rubber hose with holes every few inches, and into the hose you install a little drip mechanism. The hose is strategically placed around my acreage to drip water into the base of the various plants. Initially, I laid hundreds of feet of this hose all over my acreage on the top of the ground to accommodate my plants. So there it was; I had my state of the art irrigation system.

Apart from sand and arid conditions in the desert, we also have rabbits. Many, many, many rabbits. The majority of these rabbits are enormous creatures, with real long ears, big bodies and huge teeth. But I never really gave these things much thought because I did not have anything that they could want. That is, until I installed my irrigation system. It so happened that rabbits eat rubber. I did not know this. I always imagined that rabbits only ate vegetable matter, like carrots, and celery, or whatever. I was wrong. Rabbits prefer to thrive on a steady diet of black hose rubber. Apparently, during the dark of night, thousands of hungry rabbits would sneak up to my property and munch on my rubber hose leaving zillions of holes.

The next morning, I would go out and turn my water on, and it would look like a Roman fountain spritzing water up into the air and everywhere. I would get so angry at these rabbits. I would get so angry that I finally would go out in the morning and throw rocks at these lousy rabbits, and try to figure out how to stop them from eating through the rubber. For a while there, I got a little scared because I thought these crazy rabbits would chew the tires off my car. Eventually, I theorized that it was not the rubber that these rabbits were so intent on consuming. It was the mineral deposits on the inside of the hose from the water passing through. These rabbits craved the mineral deposits. Well, the whole thing turned into a full- scale war.

My first counter strategy was to bury my drip line. This was no easy task. I had to dig a trench hundreds of feet long all over my property to accommodate this drip line. Unfortunately, part of the drip line still needed to come to the surface in order to irrigate my trees, bushes, and so forth. After a short while, the rabbits figured out that all they needed to do was to go to my trees and such to consume the rubber hose right where it came out of the ground. Naturally, in the morning, when I would turn on the water there would be another series of Roman fountains spritzing everywhere. My anger elevated. I tried to imagine what I could do to counter these pesky rabbits right there at my plants to prevent them from eating the hose. I could not figure out a way to handle the situation for a long time.

In the meantime, we began a ritual. It was like something out of an Alfred Hitchcock movie. Every morning, I would go outside and be greeted by all these rabbits all lined up around the perimeter of my property, as though they were waiting for me. And I would go out and pick up rocks and throw them at the rabbits. To this day, I still engage in this unfulfilling activity. The good part of this is that the rabbits are no longer eating my rubber hose. But I still have to be vigilant and try to pelt them with rocks. I say *try* to pelt them with rocks, because I rarely hit them. And not because I'm such a bad shot either. Somehow they must have the capacity to calculate a trajectory, and will only move if they are certain the rock will hit them. Otherwise, they sit there, very still, with their big ears twitching, watching a rock whiz past them. Finally, I began to get philosophical about this and asked myself, "Why are they here?" I concluded that they like the ritual. Of course, they might be trying to figure out what's next or how they can get me.

Eventually, I shared with my listeners on Coast to Coast AM that I had this challenge with these rabbits. One caller asked me if I ever tried to chew aluminum foil. Of course, when I heard this I immediately thought of the sort of electric shock you get when your teeth react to the aluminum. That was the trick: I would wrap the hose at the base of my trees, and shrubs, and whatever with aluminum foil. I foiled the rabbits, so to speak. They cannot get to my hose, but for some reason, the rabbits still come. So every morning, as the sun comes up after I get off the air, I am outside collecting rocks. And then I throw them at the rabbits.

Friends

Despite my tendency to live what some people consider to be a reclusive life, I do have some close friends. I must admit, though, that most of my friends are weird people. When I say weird, it is in a kindly way. Lynn Witlake is an example of one of my very dear, lifelong friends. Lynn, as I mentioned earlier, is someone I got to know while I was in the Air Force. He is one of the guys who participated with me in creating an illegal radio station on Amarillo Air Force base and is the nut who enjoyed chasing tornadoes. Lynn is an intense, driven person, just like me. In fact, most of my closest, oldest friends are intense, driven people just like me. I suppose that is the type of person I would be most naturally drawn to, and who is drawn to me. Did I mention that my friends are weird?

Needless to say, many of my friends, perhaps most of my friends, have been in the broadcasting business. Generally, I have found that broadcasting people are driven, focused, and often very weird people. Ron Shaw is one of my long time broadcast colleagues. Ron and I met at KUDE, a radio station in Oceanside, California. At that time, I was the chief engineer at KUDE. That was a remarkable, very progressive radio station. I have known Ron for over 25 years. Ron is a hyperactive person and an absolutely devoted radio personality. Radio has been his major focus from the beginning, and still is. He always put his unbelievable energy into radio. He talks about a thousand miles an hour, but everything relates to radio in some way. The last time we visited together, I was reminded how much we had in common, and how much I really like him.

And generally, I try to associate myself with exceptional people. I do *not* tolerate fools, boring or average people, or people who just are unable to remain focused in a particular train of thought. I just don't have time for these types of people. I become impatient with them, and just intolerant of them. As for friends, I don't have any friends who are fools and try to avoid them in business. In the past, I inadvertently did business with a series of fools. At this point in my life, however, I have been very fortunate to have weeded out the fools and surrounded myself with some very talented people.

Alan Corbeth

One of my current best friends is my boss, Alan Corbeth, President of Chancellor Broadcasting Company. Alan fits into the category of people who are inclined to be my friends. He is brilliant and driven, he is ambitious without being greedy, and highly adept at recognizing and promoting talent. I admire him and respect him. I believe we are cut from the same cloth: we're hard workers, we're achievers, and we're driven to do what we do. Rather than money as the focus for what we do, it is achievement. I appreciate Alan Corbeth's professionalism, I appreciate his drive, I appreciate the fact that he is logical, I appreciate him for the man that he is on both a personal and a professional basis. This all may sound like I'm kissing Alan's butt because he's my boss, but I'm not. And if it comes out that way, who cares!

The Magic Carpet

As a child, I was perhaps five or six, one of my best friends in the whole world was Tony Watson. Tony and I would play what we called magic carpet. We would get an oval or rectangular shaped shag carpet and put this on the floor. Then we would get a fan and place it at one end of the carpet. We manufactured controls, switches, and buttons, and we would imagine that we were flying on this magic carpet. The fan would blow in our faces and we used the controls to become airborne. We would fly over the city, over houses, and over roads. We played this game for hours.

Overall, I enjoy being in the company of people who are well rounded, intelligent, knowledgeable (most likely more knowledgeable than I am), interesting, logical, driven, and ambitious. Sometimes I have been drawn to people who are veritable geniuses, maybe on the verge of madness. This may sound like a strange and unusual mix of people, but then I don't prefer to spend much time with just anyone, especially since I spend so little time with people in a social atmosphere.

Money

While growing up, my family was comfortably middle class and we never really went without anything. In the last few years, I have finally reached a point where I live comfortably. As far as the amount of money, I am sufficiently well off not to have to worry about money again in this lifetime. I suppose that this is the mark of a successful radio talk show host and it is true that I make more now than I ever have. But from my perspective, once you make enough to be comfortable, the rest is just gravy and I don't have any plans for drastically changing my lifestyle.

While I am not particularly extravagant, I have traveled the world, own a comfortable home, have several cars, and all the electronic gadgets I want. Beyond that, my use of money is superfluous, except possibly in saving for retirement, which I'm just beginning to do. There are far more interesting things to do with my time than to be preoccupied with trying to find ways to get more money. I suppose I am rather cavalier about money, especially for one who professes to be a capitalist. I care far more about my profession than the money I get. In fact, sometimes when I receive a paycheck, I just shake my head in wonder as I marvel at being paid to do something I love. It is the best of all worlds, to do what you love and make decent money doing it.

The only time I really gave much thought about money was when I did not have enough of it. There were times when I had virtually so little money, it was a challenge to buy enough food. I lived this way for years. There are many, many people in broadcasting who make very little money. It is a tough business in which to make it big, and really start making a decent living. Those who love the broadcasting business are the ones who stay with it, but not for the money. It's just not that easy to succeed. These days, with my success, the money is coming. And this is almost magical to me. And I am grateful for it. But money has never been my motive to stay in the broadcasting business, and it never will be. Money has certainly come to me because of what I do and that's wonderful. Otherwise, money is not that important to me.

Panic Attacks

One part of my life no one would really know about unless they worked with me, or unless you were my wife and had to put up with me has to do with panic attacks. What is a panic attack? A panic attack, which some may refer to as an anxiety attack, is intense physical, emotional, and mental distress which in my case is almost always related to my radio program. I began to have panic attacks when I began a regular talk radio program. I remember the first time I was about to go on the air to do a program on a Las Vegas station. My heart immediately began to race, adrenaline shot through my system, I became flush and hot, sweating like a pig — all this, just *before* the show started! On the air, I was a nervous wreck, and probably sounded like a nervous wreck. Naturally, I would grab for a cigarette and smoke myself through the worst of it. After the show was underway, I would calm down, though I often sat around with a shirt that is sopping wet with perspiration.

It may seem odd, but even after all these years of doing a live talk radio program, I still have a panic attack almost every time I'm about to go on the air. Some entertainers call them pre-stage butterflies. For me, they are huge, wet butterflies. But, every time, it goes away as I proceed with the show. Of course, I have gotten so good at disguising the fact that I'm having a panic attack that most people would never detect it.

I know when I have a good night on the air or when I have a bad night. Fortunately, most of my shows are good, so I have good nights. But every once in a while I'll have an average night. Sometimes a show can go wrong because of the way callers are responding to me. I may have misinterpreted something they said, or perhaps the caller misinterpreted something I had said. I never know what to expect because I do not screen calls.

When the show has rough spots, I can hover around the edges of a panic attack. Moreover, when this happens, it is not uncommon for a show to be average all the way through. To make matters worse, the next day, I will think of the old show business adage, "You're only as good as your last show." Yes, panic attacks are a real part of what I do, and can have a direct effect on my life. Yet perhaps if I didn't go through this ritualistic bout with adrenaline, I wouldn't feel normal!

Books

I am an avid book consumer. I love to read, I always have, and I always will. I have an extensive personal library. I read so much non-fiction in the form of periodicals, like various newspapers, magazines, and many, many faxes I receive from a variety of sources including several newswires that it is a welcome relief to escape into fiction. My tastes in fiction are varied but I tend to concentrate on contemporary thrillers. I can't really say I have one or two authors I like to read in particular, although I am an avid Stephen King reader and a Tom Clancy reader. I loved King's *The Stand*, about a virus that kills the majority of the world and how those few who survive come to terms with their situation. I also love techno-thrillers, so I love much of what Tom Clancy writes, particularly *Hunt For Red October*, the story about a Russian submarine commander who attempts to defect.

I like science fiction only when it is within the realm of possibility, such as Arthur C. Clarke's *2001: A Space Odyssey* (the movie version of this book is quite good, too). I am interested in books that have a basic grounding in science and then extend that science into science fiction. I am not a hard core science fiction fan at all and not fantasy either. I hate that swords and sorcerers stuff.

Among other books I have enjoyed reading include Nevil Shute's *On the Beach*, a novel about the end of the world; Orson

Scott Card's *Speaker For the Dead*, which I thought was an absolute masterpiece; Whitley Strieber's *War Day*, and Martin Gross's *The Red President*. A particularly exceptional book was *Lucifer's Hammer*, by Larry Niven and Jerry Pournelle, ironically enough the story of a comet on a collision course with earth.

I was particularly impressed with Richard Preston's page-turner, *The Hot Zone*, a tale of Ebola virus run rampant. Not only was this based on a true story, but I also feel that it could happen again in the near future. Preston's gripping, often gory descriptions of the power of the Ebola virus combined with his ability to tell a good, solid story made this one of my faster recent reads.

Sometimes the books I am most impressed by are not necessarily by the biggest, best-selling authors. For instance, I recently read Michael Cordy's book, *The Miracle Strain*. His book deals with a man who has invented a machine that can decode the genetic blueprint of man and basically predict the nature of that man's life physically. His wife is killed by someone whose intention it was to get her inventor husband out of the way, and later his daughter is struck with a terminal disease. The majority of the book combines technology with a sacred quest, a natural thriller that kept me hooked the whole way through.

Movies

I am also an avid movie watcher and video collector. Again, my interests in movies are a broad mixture. I do avoid musicals because I hate them. I don't go out of my way to watch violence in a movie, and if it is in a movie and doesn't move the plot forward, but is just gratuitous, I turn it off. I could never sit and watch one of those stupid kung fu movies where 500 people die or something shallow like that. I'm not crazy about baseball, but I love several excellent baseball movies. The best baseball movies I have seen include *Field of Dreams* with Kevin Costner, *Major League* with Tom Berenger and Charlie Sheen, and *Damn Yankees* with Jean Stapleton.

Some of the movies I like reflect my fascination with technology, for instance, *The Bedford Incident*, made in 1965, which is the story of a Navy captain scouting Russian subs near Greenland and the mental conflicts aboard his ship. With stars like Sidney Poitier and Richard Widmark, it is easy to become engrossed in a movie that was, at the time, so relevant to the Cold War. *Seven Days in May* is an absorbing, believable story of a military scheme to overthrow the government that I also enjoyed.

I was highly impressed by the recent version of *Titanic*. I think I have seen it three times. The special effects are not what make the movie, although that is a definite enhancement; the story is enough to carry me and even the love story was superb. I interviewed a survivor of the Titanic on Coast to Coast. This lady was in lifeboat 13 and she sat listening to the screams of the people. Between the movie and this interview, the Titanic experience has been an intense one for me.

The controversial film *Amistad* was also of interest to me. It was the kickoff to the Civil War in America, so the issues of slavery were right at the forefront. These slaves were of unknown origin and the case went all the way to the Supreme Court. I think that case caused a lot of people to begin to consider the way they viewed slavery. Stephen Spielberg has recently followed a trend of making movies that are intellectually stimulating and provocative. And this one is no exception; it should make even today's society stop and think about our past and the way we viewed and thought of the whole slavery issue.

I love Anthony Hopkins; I think he is an outstanding actor. So it was no surprise that I enjoyed the taut suspense and gripping story line of *The Edge*. Some of the reviews for the movie were not glowing, but the reviewers were wrong. I think it may have been Hopkins' best performance ever. You also have to realize that he usually plays dark, small character roles, but this was a movie in which he was front and center. Anthony Hopkins reminds me of Richard Burton in a way, especially with their Welsh backgrounds. Hopkins is so quietly authoritative and sophisticated that I have been consistently impressed with him throughout his career and this movie is no exception.

Also along the lines of more recent movies is a picture called *The Rapture*. Now, this film has a reputation for controversy and of course, as with everything, might not suit many people's taste. Mimi Rogers stars as a woman who becomes fanatically religious; there are overtones of apocalypse throughout the film, but I think one of the reasons I like it is that it rushes in where some fear to tread and that seems to fit my mindset in many ways.

Sports

Most sports to me are a crushing, crashing bore. Baseball is a slow, painful thing to watch, and even more painful to listen to. I object to it on the grounds that frequently it will drag out and many times even pre-empt my radio program. You have the Dodgers in a 22-inning slugfest, and they'll go till two o'clock in the morning and that pre-empts my show. So, my overall comment about baseball is that: a) It's boring to watch; b) It's more boring to listen to; and c) It's frustrating when it pre-empts my program. What else is boring to me? It's a long boring list. Hockey is boring, basketball is boring, etc., etc. Listening to basketball on the radio really defies understanding. All you hear is the squeak of sneakers all the time going up and down, going back and forth and back and forth. I guess there is excitement in it for some people.

The one sport I do love is football. I love to sit in front of my big TV with my surround-sound audio system blasting and watch as much of the game as I can. Football is a bone-crunching, one-on-one, direct kind of man's game which may say something about my testosterone level, I don't know. But I love football, and do not make any apologies for it. And when football season begins, for me, life begins. Football becomes an integral part of my personal life at that point. I follow football, I bet on football. Thank goodness I live in a state where betting on football is legal. So I put down ten bucks and bet on a game. That's about all I have to say about sports.

Fantasy

I am not a man with a lot of unfulfilled fantasies. When I was young, I dreamed of being behind the microphone at a station with 50,000 watts— and I have. I was overcome with the fantasy of travel, an insatiable wanderlust — and I have traversed the world now several times over. But the one great fantasy that still remains with me to this day is my desire to fly.

Ever since I was a boy, I have had this longing to fly. As I have described earlier, I made a number of attempts at flight. I employed umbrellas and I even considered constructing a wing with the intent to launch myself into flight (fortunately my Mom stopped me before I got any further with this one). Years later, as an adult, when I was doing a show for KENI in Anchorage, Alaska (one of my current affiliates, by the way), I was coerced into trying hang gliding. It wasn't too hard to convince me; I am and probably always will be a kid at heart and so the idea appealed to me. I was supposed to demonstrate the first time use of a hang glider as a radio promotional event.

The hang glider was provided by a man who owned a hang gliding shop and was an expert in hang gliding. I sat down with the guy beforehand and said, "Look, what are the chances of my getting hurt here?"

And he said, "Nothing, literally, nothing can go wrong. Trust me. Nothing can go wrong." He explained that I would glide in the air for about 15 or 20 seconds, close to the earth, and then land again.

So, having been sold on the idea, and very much wanting to fly, I showed up at the site where this event would occur: Palmer, Alaska, a remote rural part of Alaska, a two-hour trip from Anchorage. It was a typical summer day and a big crowd had gathered to watch Art Bell hang glide.

I eagerly strapped myself into this hang glider. Then, just as I had been carefully instructed, I hoisted the hang glider above me and ran like hell down a hill. And, I flew! — for about five seconds. And it was the most wonderful, exhilarating, tremendous feeling I have ever had in my life. Then, just as I was nearing my point of touchdown, a violent crosswind caught hold of the glider, and, as easily as a child throws a plate from its high chair to the ground, flipped it over. An aluminum arm on the hang glider came down on top of my arm and crushed it to the ground, as easily as a pretzel.

They put a big splint on me and I had a bone jiggling around and they drove me over this rutted road toward Anchorage. Every time we hit a hole in the road, I was in absolute agony. Everyone who was at the scene of my crash donated some type of drug to me to relieve me of my pain. In fact, I was given so many drugs that by the time I arrived at the hospital in Anchorage, the doctor took one look at me and asked, "How can you possibly be conscious?" My arm was compound fractured two inches above the elbow, the worst place to break your arm. It was such a bad break that the attending nurse took one look at me and passed out. Not only did I have to wear a huge, cumbersome cast, I also spent six weeks sleeping in a chair, wearing only cut up t-shirts; you had to cut them up to get them on me. I even went back to work and did a one-armed show at KENI. This was my worst flying experience.

I Still Dream of Flying

If you were wondering, I have not learned my lesson. The desire to fly still courses through me. In fact, one of the best dreams I have had while sleeping was about flying. To begin with, I normally do not dream very often, or I at least do not recall many dreams I may have. The dreams I do remember are normally in black and white. Rarely do I have a dream in color. Well, I had this one dream of flying, and it was not only in brilliant, gorgeous color, but it was one of the most wonderful flights I could ever imagine. I was on the top of the Empire State building and someone had sprinkled me with pixie dust, and I was immediately able to float over New York City, in and around the buildings. It was amazing. I don't know what it means, if anything, but I don't pretend to know how to interpret dreams. Perhaps it is because I am so preoccupied with flying. I don't know.

If I had my life to live all over again, I would probably become a pilot. These days I am contemplating getting a pilot's license, or at the very least I'm getting serious about buying for myself a powered hang glider. I have watched many people fly powered hang gliders over Pahrump Valley and I long to do what they are doing. It seems to be the safest, easiest, and the closest way to the way I want to fly, like a bird. I am aware of the risks, of the sudden change in winds, or something else beyond my control. I am aware that I could risk my life just to have this experience of flight. But sometimes, it may be worth the risk to do certain things in life. My wife, of course, does not like this idea, and she is one of a long line of people who don't want me to fly. But I believe that flying is something no one can really prevent me from doing. It is just the one fantasy I must satisfy.

Regrets

When I sat down to think about my life, I discovered how difficult and painful it was to reflect on my regrets. The human brain, I believe, in protection of itself, tends to fog over and forget events that one finds too difficult to remember. But when making a record of your life, as in the case of this book, people want to know, and as painful as this may be, I feel I have an obligation to tell the truth.

People

One of the foremost regrets in my life is that I did not treat people better. When I was young, I was foolish and frequently I treated people poorly. Some of the people I mistreated were women. Yes, I know earlier I indicated how much I love women, but for some reason, I did not treat some women very well. For one thing, I had what you might call 'shallow' relationships with women. I can remember dating women who fell in love with me, and I did not reciprocate that love. Instead, I was selfish, and took from the relationship; I, in essence, used these women. I am very ashamed for my attitude and my behavior of when I was young. At my age now, I realize how cruel and cold that can be. I regret my behavior and I have guilt about it to this day.

Business

I have also taken advantage of people I have done business with in the past. To some degree, a business relationship often involves taking advantage of people on both sides: the employer uses the employee and the employee uses the employer. But I know I treated some of my employers poorly, particularly in the many years I spent in broadcasting, in many small radio stations. I was an egotistical, angry young man, and many times I did not show appropriate respect to those older and wiser than I was.

Smoking

My second greatest regret is that I ever began smoking cigarettes. I smoked my first cigarette when I was 16 years old, and at this writing, I just turned 53. That's 34 long years smoking every day. That's tens of thousands of cigarettes. And I still smoke, although I am very much aware about the hazards of smoking. Even though it is a bad habit I have adopted, it is a tough one to kick. It's a strange thing, but many people in radio broadcasting are consummate cigarette smokers. Smoking becomes a nervous habit that you adopt to take the edge off the tension of performing in broadcasting. I have nothing against people who smoke because what other people do is their own business, but I do regret that I have not mustered the will power to stop smoking. I have tried many times, but no matter what I try—the patch, pills, whatever—I just cannot quit.

I regret, apart from the havoc smoking has undoubtedly wreaked on my body, that I did not take better care of myself. I have not really had the best of eating habits and I do not like exercise. I think of what the late great Mickey Mantle repeated recently, "If I had known I would live this long, I would have taken better care of myself." And that's true of me too. Some of us do foolish things in our youth. In our foolishness, we think we are immortal. So we do the things which we ought not to do.

My Father

I regret that my father and I were not closer. We were not close as I grew up. Perhaps given the nature of my parents' relationship, it is no surprise that there is a great distance between my father and I. Some things you can forgive, but you cannot remove their imprint from your soul. To this day, I have what I would call a cordial relationship with my father. It is much better than it used to be but the relationship is still only cordial.

Japan

I have tremendous regret and bear some guilt about a Japanese woman with whom I lived in Japan. In effect, I lived as a Japanese person would live in Japan. After several years, she progressively developed a mental illness. It started with a mental breakdown, and she became paranoid and schizophrenic. She began to hear things, she began to see things. She began to lose touch with reality. Eventually, her condition became so serious she did not even know who I was. I stayed with her for years, and this was very sad. I was frustrated and sad because I was powerless. This was especially difficult for someone like me because I'm the type of person who wants power over things, and this was a situation over which I had no power or influence in any way. But I tried. She was in and out of mental health institutions, in and out of trouble, and in and out of sanity. Finally she went completely insane. None of the doctors who examined her could come up with an explanation.

Whether her insanity stemmed from a chemical brain imbalance or some other disorder no one seemed to know. I realized there was nothing left for me to do but to leave Japan. Which I did, leaving her behind. She is now most likely still in Japan, and most likely in an institution. It has been years since I have heard about her. My guess is that she has not recovered.

My Technical World

I have some regret that I have spent my life in a technical world. Technical things are a passion for me. And to some degree, my interest in technical things has had an effect on my success. But there have been so many times when I passed up a variety of social opportunities that I think would have broadened me. This is a part of life that I think is unfortunate I have missed. I believe this problem often occurs to academics, entrepreneurs, and to those who are generally driven, or are of a one-track mind. I will stick with a technical project doggedly until I have either solved it or so totally ruined it that it is beyond redemption. I have usually done this at the expense of everything else, especially any possibility of a social life.

And yet I believe this same drive has been the reason for success in my life. Being a driven person is very much a two-edged sword. People driven are into what they do, and sometimes they end up not being very gregarious. Somehow, I feel it is possible to miss out by avoiding interaction with people in social settings.

Friendships

I regret not having sustained enduring friendships over the years. When I grew up, it was virtually impossible to make friends, because my family moved around so often. And it so happened that my life in broadcasting was not much different. Many people in the business will tell you what a gypsy sort of life it is. You go from town to town or city to city as you go from one radio station to another. Every move means having to re-assimilate to a new culture, find a new place to live, learn where to shop, meet a new set of people. And any meaningful relationships you make during your sojourn in a given place are almost surely lost when you move again. Promises of writing to each other are made, but almost never kept. A month goes by, then six months, and then a year. Years slip by and those relationships are lost. This is sad, and I regret allowing some past relationships to disappear.

Spirituality

I regret I cannot satisfy my spiritual longing. I have investigated many religions and spiritual ways of thinking, but nothing yet seems to fulfill me spiritually. As a youngster, I was baptized a Lutheran, and I went to church for a while, but eventually never went back. I do not need to go to a church every Sunday, and have someone support my belief system. Nor do I feel the need to denigrate in any way those who do go to church.

Now, I believe we have a maker, that there is a God. But I am the sort of person who wants proof. I need to put my hands on things, to establish in some way for myself that something *is*. I also want to be assured that there is a life after this one. One big problem I have, I suppose, is that I am unable to accept things on faith. I have great respect for people who can accept things on faith. I would never belittle people who have faith. I have discovered that in any religious discussion, it always comes down to one thing: having faith. I cannot accept what structured religion teaches because so much of it depends entirely on faith.

I am a pragmatist. So far, the only faith I have is in what I can see, or understand — mostly technical or scientifically supported things. My popular radio program, *Dreamland* is an extension of my personal interest in learning about spiritual matters. I am open and still interested in learning all I can about these topics. That's why I will talk about and listen to people who investigate the paranormal, near death experiences, the possibility of an afterlife, reincarnation, hypnosis, and so on.

Recently, in very non-traditional religious ways, I have become more spiritual. I didn't suddenly run down to church and I still am

89

not doing that. Rather, I would say that I hold reincarnationist beliefs. I believe you have to be responsible for the issues in your life, and that if you, in essence, try to escape that responsibility by suicide, the same problems will come back the next time around. In a personal sense, my spirituality is centered on matters of the spirit, the afterlife, and the fact that we're probably more than just a big bag of water and chemicals.

In the end, I think everything probably balances out. Without regrets, perhaps I would not be able to truly appreciate the good things in my life, the achievements I have made. And the fact remains that you cannot change what has already been forged; you can only try to live the best life you can day by day.

Politics

I have very mixed political views. My popular radio colleague, Rush Limbaugh is fond of telling his listeners: "You don't need to read the papers, or watch or listen to the news; all you need to know, I will give to you." I never make such a boast because I want people to think for themselves. I think for myself and I offer my views for my listeners to consider, and in the end, they can think for themselves. Rush Limbaugh runs exclusively along Republican lines. But I am a big political mixture, which on the whole is mostly Libertarian, but not exclusively. I listen to everyone: Republicans, Democrats, and Libertarians. I weigh everything, and then decide for myself what I believe is right. That's how I am, that's how I encourage my listeners to be.

As of this writing, I'm about to join the Libertarian party. I don't agree with them on everything, but I agree on more than not. I don't know that anyone everyone agrees with a group completely, but I'm presently registered Republican and the critical mass of disagreement with them has been reached. I want to have an affiliation with the group that I feel most closely reflects what I believe and that is the Libertarian party. And if I have disagreements with some of their policies the best way to try and modify them is to be on the inside not the outside.

A Libertarian Life

What does it mean for me to be a Libertarian? Generally, a Libertarian is someone who believes that for the most part people have the right to their own personal realm. For instance, Libertarians believe (and I don't completely share this belief) that, as an example, if you want to do drugs in your own home, it's your business. And unless your actions affect someone else, Libertarians are in favor of smaller, less intrusive government. They hold to a philosophy of personal liberties and pretty much leaving the other guy alone unless he bothers you. It's live and let live.

I have my own personal views and I separate those from what I feel politically about how intrusive government ought to be in private life. In other words, I work for a very large corporation and I don't piss in jars and I don't give blood samples. I think that is very intrusive, particularly now when you give a blood sample and they can do a DNA workup on you and they can know more about you than you know about you. That's an invasion of privacy.

My Politics Started Young

So where did my political views come from? Politics is something I began to focus on when I was about thirteen or fourteen. I read a pamphlet from the John Birch Society, but decided that it was too radical for me. Later, I was a supporter of the Goldwater presidential campaign. Politics is generally a topic that people like to talk about. Rush spends practically all of his time talking politics. This is fine, for him. For me, I can talk politics with the best of them, but I do not limit myself to just politics; there are many other interesting topics to discuss and I discuss them.

Nonetheless, early on in this business, I recognized the keen interest in politics many listeners have, and I have sought to accommodate them. But I did grow up in an environment where politics were brought up. My mother is a conservative. My father was once very conservative, but is now very liberal. I am somewhere in between, probably leaning more towards my mom's political ideology. There are a number of issues in America today, which define what people are politically. My stance on some of these issues reveals where I am politically.

One Issue at a Time

When it comes to politics, what I do is take each issue as it comes along. There have been rare moments when I have even agreed with Bill Clinton. For example, at one point, Clinton took a hard stand against the Japanese about their trade practices. I'm tired of being screwed by the Japanese, even though I think they are wonderful people, and I love their country and their culture. But their trade policies tend to be in the same vein as their culture and that is homogeneous. Japanese generally prefer to do business with other Japanese and not foreigners unless it is to their own benefit.

Thus, it is no surprise that for years, in the automobile business, the Japanese employed the "old boy" system of keeping American cars and parts out of the competition by simply not pushing them at all. There is, of course, no specific law in Japan that prohibits America from doing business there; conversely, there is no law and no way to make a law that forces the Japanese to use American parts, etc.

So, when President Clinton threatened to place a 200 percent import duty on their luxury cars, I was in agreement with him. Unfortunately, at the last moment, Clinton wimped out and didn't do anything. Still, this is an example of when I supported this Democrat President when he at least seemed to want to do something good for our country. I finally believed the monster from our id had taken a good, strong position; I was disappointed when he didn't follow through. Nonetheless, the point is that I take each issue individually, and make an honest assessment of an issue. I am honest with myself and I am honest with my listeners. And I do not make a judgment based only on my mostly Libertarian political tendencies. I am a Libertarian naturally; my political persuasion is not manufactured. I also do not try to persuade my listeners in any particular way; I let them draw their own conclusions.

The Nature of Politics

I believe that in order to be a politician in America you have to be a liar. There are very few politicians who do not fall into that category. I believe to get elected in America, you must have the kind of talent Bill Clinton has. That talent is to be able to tell people exactly what they want to hear. I call him "the mighty morphin-man;" he's like a chameleon. I believe it was one of Clinton's own political advisors who said that when asked a question, Clinton automatically envisions a poll in his mind before answering, and tries to calculate which way the wind blows. Then he will answer with the hope that he will appease most of the people who are listening to him.

Such cynicism and insincerity is frightening. But that is apparently the way you get elected and the way you maintain office in this country these days. For that reason, I would never go into politics. Otherwise, I would already have been tempted in. But I can't operate so dishonestly; I couldn't and I wouldn't. I guess that makes me sound like I have a high moral standard, though I think I have an average moral standard. But it seems that to be a politician in this country, you must have a very low moral standard, and you must be willing to lie to the American people.

Globalism & Politicians

The people I do admire I am a little gun-shy of. For example, I admire Pat Buchanan because he says exactly what's on his mind, and I believe him to be an honest man. I also believe a lot of what he says has value. Unfortunately he's too radical for me. He is an isolationist. He would close this country's borders and impose tariffs that would discourage trade into this country; he would generally ignore most of the rest of the world, and I am just not that much of an isolationist. Maybe I'm more of a realist. I have traveled a lot, and given what's going on in China, Japan, and Europe, I know we cannot afford to be isolationists.

We live in a global economy, and to ignore or avoid this is foolish. If we were to isolate ourselves, only we would be the losers as the rest of the world would pass us by. And although I admire his honesty, I am afraid of his radical nature. Another example is Bob Dornan. Again, just as with Buchanan, I respect him, and he is another politician who will say exactly what is on his mind. But if it came down to a vote, I would not vote for him; he's much too radical for me.

Why I Voted For Ross Perot

I voted for Ross Perot in the 1992 election. The reason is that I could not stomach George Bush and his broken promises (e.g., he claimed he would not raise taxes, and he did, etc.). I certainly could not handle any of the so-called alternative possibilities for President, such as Michael Dukakis. I must say, quite frankly, from the beginning, I thought Ross Perot was a little crazy, although perhaps the word 'eccentric' is more accurate. However, he is exactly what they needed in Washington. There really is not more than a dime's worth of difference between any of the people who try for the next shot at the presidency.

Now don't get me wrong, there is a great deal of difference between the beliefs of a conservative and a liberal. Usually, during the course of a campaign, there may seem to be vast differences among candidates, but once they are elected, regardless of which side they are coming from, they look very much the same. Why? Because they generally serve much the same master or masters. This is not necessarily a belief on my part in a conspiracy by a hidden hand such as the Trilateral Commission, the Council on Foreign Relations, the Rockefellers, or whoever else people often believe controls what goes on. It is just that the average person taking the office of President, no matter what they have said during the campaign, bows to certain realities in Washington.

The one person who would not have bowed like others would have been Ross Perot. He might not have lasted long, but he would have shaken up those people in Washington like never before. And his doing so would have been a healthy thing. So, with this in mind, and on a wing and a prayer, I voted for Ross Perot. To this day, I am not sorry, nor do I regret doing it.

Approach with an Open Mind

I truly am in the middle in a lot of ways. I am not a radical on either the left or the right. Sometimes that is just not a good populist place to be. People love the Buchanans, they love the Dornans, and these Buchanan and Dornan admirers tend to deplore those who are in the middle. Some people may think my middle of the road position just makes me a bunch of mush. I don't think so. I think my opinions are the opinions of a majority of people in America today. I generally approach issues with an open mind and not purely from an ideological base. I also try to approach issues with an intellectual perspective and careful consideration.

To illustrate what a mixture I can be politically, I must admit that I even admire and respect politicians who are democratic. Sam Nunn, for example, who is honest, pragmatic, and intelligent, is someone who I would vote for if he ran for President. I'm sure this will shock many of my listeners and readers. Open minded and thoughtful, that's what I hope to be, that's what I try to be, and that's what I try to convey to my listeners on the air. I'm glad that there is room on radio for someone with my political views.

Abortion

This is probably the most divisive issue in America today. I believe the embryo in a woman's womb is life. In other words, when there is that unique genetic mixture, life has begun. My stand on abortion is that I am personally opposed to it, but I am not about to tell someone down the street what they can or can't do with their own body. I also don't think that the government has any business doing that either.

My pro-life view is personal, but I am pro-choice for anyone else because I believe it is the business of the person who is carrying the child. But I'm not a fanatic, nor am I dogmatic about my position. I don't march in front of abortion clinics and I don't encourage people to do this. Instead, I simply make it clear that the 1.5 million or so abortions that have occurred in this country are a sin, an absolutely undeniable sin. And I even think most of the people who call themselves pro-choice know this. In their hearts, they know it.

I also feel that the man should have some say in what happens to an unborn child, too, because he is half the creation process. No, he doesn't have to carry the child for nine months, but I think many people simply ignore the fact that fathers have an interest in this issue as well.

To me, the answer to the abortion debate in America is not whether or not we should have abortion clinics. After all, people will just go with their coat hangers and perform their own abortions. The answer to abortion is birth control. It's never being faced with the decision of whether to destroy life, and to carry the guilt that such a decision may create. I know that many women are haunted by the choice they made to destroy life. It is a profound and serious decision to be confronted with and abortions themselves are not pretty things. This is why I am adamant about birth control.

The biggest obstacle to my suggested solution is the Catholic Church. The Catholic religion has its aspects of beauty. Of course, I am not religious, but I have made a concerted effort to learn about many, many religions. As I see it, the problem with the Catholic Church is that it preaches against birth control. And because Catholicism is still so influential in the world today, many people are affected. So, I think the Catholic Church is somewhat blind in their view of this issue; I think birth control should be provided for anyone who needs it. This could be the ultimate answer to the argument between people who march in front of the clinics and those who say every woman should have a choice. I just

96

say every woman ought not to have to make that choice. She should have birth control. What does this make me? A pro-life, moderate, if there is such a thing.

Besides a solution of birth control for everyone, which is probably not that realistic, I would suggest that at the very least, people who have an opportunity to choose what course of action they will take should think about children before becoming intimate. Additionally, people who are the victims of violent crimes should not feel afraid to make the choice that is best for them at the time, instead of being intimidated into a decision by demonstrators or coerced by well-meaning parents. Having a child or having an abortion both carry long term effects mentally and the choice needs to exist.

The Right to Die

More and more, this is becoming a divisive issue in this country, although probably not as much as abortion. Personally, I would want it to be an option for others, but I wouldn't do it for spiritual reasons. It is my view that you have to work out what you have to work out in this life and that if you don't work it out this time, you will have to work it out next time.

Oregon was the first state to make it legal for a doctor to prescribe a lethal drug to a patient who wanted the choice of death. I think it won't be long before other states follow suit. People argue the morality of taking life, but morality doesn't have a goddamn thing to do with it and shouldn't as far as the government is concerned. You know the theory of whose life is it anyway, and all that. But these kinds of issues, abortion and the right to die, should not be part of the government's realm.

America's Economy

I am an economic Libertarian; I believe in the work ethic, capitalism, free enterprise, etc. I agreed with Ross Perot about this country's debt. America is in enormous debt and continues to fall into greater debt. At some point, perhaps five or ten years, this debt is going to come cascading down on our heads. This debt is going to catch up with us. I personally could not go into debt, indefinitely, without going bankrupt. Likewise, America cannot continue to go into debt at the present rate without going bankrupt. This may sound strange and cynical to think that America, a country that was once one of the economic powerhouses of the world could go bankrupt, but it is an inevitable reality. And when this country goes bankrupt, not 'if' it goes bankrupt, but *when* it goes bankrupt, a lot of people are going to be hurt.

Americans are accustomed to a very comfortable, convenient, self-indulgent lifestyle. We are spoiled in this country. In short, America has become soft. We have had it too good, for too long. When we face an economic emergency, it will probably be coupled with a social emergency. It will be unlike anything anyone has ever seen, and many people will not be able to endure. There will be riots, there will be panic, there will be hunger, and there will be an America torn apart as never before. We are not ready for such difficult times. We are a soft people, and even I admit I may be one of the soft ones. But I recognize intellectually what is happening and I am preparing for what I believe is an inevitable catastrophe.

I remember a movie called *The High and Mighty* about an aircraft going across the Atlantic Ocean to England from America, as they do today daily. Only in this case, the make of the aircraft could not accommodate a fuel reserve. So, there was a point while going over the Atlantic that this aircraft could not turn back if something went wrong, but had to continue going forward with the available fuel. The Atlantic plane trip quite literally had a point of no return. I believe, economically, we have passed the point of no return.

I believe everyone should prepare personally. That does not mean running out and joining someone's militia, or donning fatigues and waiting for Armageddon. I believe it means taking good common sense steps to prepare. As best you can, get out of debt. As best you can, become independent in every way possible. To prepare myself for what is to come, I am personally out of debt. Fortunately, I make more money now than I ever have, and this has helped me get and stay out of debt, as well as being able to save money.

Taxes

There has been more and more talk recently about how out of control the Internal Revenue Service has gotten. Cases have come out in the open where the IRS has intimidated former spouses in an attempt to collect on a debt that the other person is responsible for. In a country as advanced as ours, we have not progressed in this area. It's time to trash the present system and change to some form of flat tax, based on a percentage, 14% or 10%, whatever it takes to make it revenue neutral so that we don't lose money. If we would realign the present system and make it fair so everyone paid the same percentage, not higher percentages for people who make more, but an even percentage. I don't know what that magic percentage will turn out to be, but it has to be revenue neutral so that it doesn't change what the government receives in terms of revenue, but I know that it would save everyone a whole lot of money. Right now we punish productivity and we punish success.

The reason for the IRS and its tax code setup is that's the only power Washington has. In other words, this is the power to tax and the power to give people breaks for whatever reason—if government wants to affect social policy, for example—if they want to affect behavior, they do it with the tax code. If you take that power away from them, they have virtually nothing else. In my opinion, they will never give that up. That is what Congress and the Senate spend their time doing: modifying the tax code, giving breaks to this business or that business, to encourage solar power or discourage solar power, or to encourage people to get married or to discourage them.

I'm not saying we shouldn't pay for the privilege of living in America or for the benefits that we receive by living in America, but it's a completely screwed up, power grubbing bureaucracy right now. Now is that going to change? In an ideal world, I would like to see a flat tax and a flat tax is absolutely possible, but what do you think is going to happen when you ask the people who run this country to give up their power?

Further, I still feel America is the best place in the world to live. I have done an extensive amount of traveling and seen a lot of different places and no matter where else you go, it only gets worse. I mean if you're talking about taxes, in Scandinavian countries for example, it's up around 60 or 80% of your income and then the government decides who gets the money distributed to them. And so that ends up in a situation where people will go to college and graduate school and become doctors and as soon as they manage to get their license, they move to New York so they can make some money.

Gun Control

I have read the Second Amendment to this country's Constitution. What is recorded there seems quite clear to me. It says very clearly, and succinctly, that Americans have the right, even a God given right, to protect themselves. This means the bearing of arms, if necessary. I am candid about revealing that I have a collection of guns. And I would not hesitate to use them to protect myself or my family. However, in America today, there are many people who do not believe we should have guns, and that the only people who should have guns are the police and the military. These anti-gun people are out of their minds. I believe Americans have a God given right to protect themselves with the same force that, in all likelihood, would be used against them.

There are a lot of bad guys running around with guns. Of course, no one can pass a law to prevent a crime and criminals would commit crimes no matter what law existed; this is just a fact of life. But, politicians do the easy thing: they blame the crime on the gun. It's easy to pass a law against a gun. Unfortunately, to the American public, this makes the politicians look like they are doing something about crime when they are not. What they are doing is taking away our God given and our Forefather given rights to self-protection. I see our rights as Americans eroding very quickly.

Why do Americans buy into these arguments made by politicians that the gun is the culprit? It is not. The gun is no more the culprit than a knife that may have been used in a killing, or a club, or a blunt instrument of some kind. Guns, knives, clubs, etc., are just material things.

I suppose that because I believe that the Second Amendment ensures that I have the right to own and bear arms, I am a Libertarian. The liberals, the ones who want to take away the guns are at best insincere, and at worst, hypocritical. Why? Because the guns are not causing the violence, it's the people who are picking them up and using them. Recently, in Africa, there were thousands of people who were killed by machetes. The sad fact is that if people wish to kill people, they will always find a way. It doesn't matter whether it's a blunt instrument or a machete or a gun. So the whole gun control thing is a red herring. It's not the guns, it's the politicians who find it beneficial to their careers to pass laws against guns. But they cannot pass laws that will stop crime, or cause people to turn from crime. Consider this: we already have gun control laws, and they are not working.

The Needy

There are people who are blind, or who are crippled, or for one physical reason or another, cannot earn a decent living. These people get a pathetic amount of money each month through social security. Most do not get more than perhaps $500 or $600 per month and, as such live generally below the poverty line. As a civilization, if that's what we want to call ourselves, we should be ashamed to provide such a pitiful amount of money for these people to live on.

Why do we allow this to go on? Because we allow so much fraud among those who take advantage of the system. There are many, many people who make false claims to receive assistance. Most claims are not investigated, because it is easier to just pay to support a bureaucracy, and the liberals who foster it, by issuing checks to anyone who makes up a story to receive those checks.

101

There are too many people who claim injury or some physical affliction they don't have. If we had all the people who are fraudulently taking money off the government payrolls, we could afford to support the truly needy in a manner that we ought to, if we want to call ourselves a civilized society.

Drugs

Many people, including conservatives like William F. Buckley, and various other notables, argue passionately for the legalization of drugs. I haven't taken that step mentally and I don't think I can because I think they are wrong. I think Mr. Buckley and others are not familiar with the tragedies caused by cocaine and other more serious drugs. However, I have long been an advocate of decriminalizing marijuana. I think, arguably, that marijuana is not as harmful as alcohol or tobacco, substances we peddle legally in this country. Right now we tell lies about it. Take a kid who is thirteen years old. He's watching commercials on television that say marijuana will fry his brains and that he'll go out and rape and pillage and plunder, then he tries marijuana and he says, geez, that's not true, then you have an even bigger problem. Because after this 13-year old is lied to, it makes the next step even easier, for instance, when he is offered crack or a line of coke.

The World Health Organization (WHO) just withheld a study that shows the marijuana is less harmful physically than cigarettes or alcohol. They covered it up. So as far as I'm concerned, marijuana probably should be decriminalized nationwide. Cocaine, crack, heroin, PCP, speed, and the other harder drugs should be treated differently, but certainly not legalized. I am not in favor of the legalization of cocaine and I know a lot of Libertarians are—and all drugs for that matter. Those drugs are serious; they ruin lives. I am not in favor of that and that is probably where I depart from a pure Libertarian and I am more a conservative.

Legalization of these serious drugs would undoubtedly produce a society of addicts we cannot support. Already, America's productivity is hurt by the drug problem we have. If drugs like cocaine and heroin are readily available, I think it would be the end of the country. And are people responsible enough to handle the legalization of a drug of any kind? Instinctively I would say, yes, but it's really a mixture. Alcohol's legal—are people responsible enough to handle that? No, it costs society $100 million a year. Marijuana would cost substantially less and would yield a bigger tax—as a matter of fact, the *New York Times* wrote an article indicating that if hemp and all its by-products were legalized, it would yield a half trillion dollars a year in revenue to the government. That's a lot of money.

So everything in perspective. If marijuana is less harmful than alcohol, then why do we keep putting people in jail for it? Sixty five percent of the people in prison are in for drugs and a healthy percentage of those are marijuana users. We are spending the larger part of the drug budget fighting marijuana not the more serious drugs. It's an insane lie of a policy and it is more harmful than good.

If we give up, if we throw up our hands and say it is the end of the drug war, as a nation we are all but washed up, ruined. For all the history we have to look at, the Chinese, the people in Holland, and so on, one might think their handling of drugs would teach us a lesson. The fact is, given free reign many people will sink into the world of drugs. It finally got so bad in China, they started putting bullets into heads of people who were addicts, and they continued to do that until they solved their drug problem.

I am an advocate of a meaningful drug war, which we do not have right now. This may mean being aggressive and burning fields in South America, or executing people who sell drugs, or executing people who import large quantities of drugs into this country, whatever it takes. The Clinton administration has done virtually nothing about the drug problem in this country. They have been very silent on the drug issue probably because they know there is little that can be done. And why draw attention to an issue that eventually would only make Clinton and his administration look bad. The drug problem in America is not going to go away; it needs to be addressed.

Ultimately, I cannot bring myself to accept the argument for the legalization of drugs in America. I think the arguments for it may be profound, but certainly not as convincing as the arguments against legalization. One argument for legalization is that it will stop the violence associated with drug traffic. Is this to suggest that a twelve or thirteen year old, who makes $500 or $1,000 a week as a lookout or a drug runner, will take a job at McDonald's flipping burgers once drug legalization occurs? Unfortunately, I think they will just resort to some other lucrative crime, which will probably still involve hurting people. Drug legalization will not make the crime go away. The crime is a larger societal problem; it is just currently centered on drugs.

Social Security

Many Libertarians, including myself, have an ideological objection to social security. I understand that the social security system will go broke at the exact year I am eligible for retirement (that is, provided they don't raise that age, which the government probably will). I have paid into social security all of my working life. Consequently, I feel that I am due what I have put in. I am certainly not one of those calling to end social security. And the government should take its rotten little hands off it. They have been stealing from the social security system for a very long time. Now they are coming back and telling us that it may survive, provided that we put more money into it. I am sorry for the burden this will put on our children; that is, if America does not suffer total financial collapse first. I definitely feel entitled to get some of my money out of it, but don't expect even one red cent.

I oppose the whole concept of social security primarily because any time you look to the government as a solution you are making a poor decision. The government has its role at making the country run efficiently, but I feel that to expect it to play a savior type of role is a mistake. The social security system has existed as settled law all my life. So, selfishly, I suppose, I'm saying I damn well better get mine, because I have contributed. What does this make me? A selfish Libertarian? I don't know. Maybe it makes me a person who is dismayed with the way the social security system has evolved into a method of encouraging dependency in America. This is supposed to be a country of enterprising self-starters, yet, as I said, more and more people are hooked to getting something for nothing from the system.

Racism

Incidentally, while I do my radio broadcast, every so often there are people who believe that because I have a combination of Libertarian and conservative views, that I am a racist. I am not. In fact, in my personal life I am part of an inter-racial marriage. But this is not something I advertise. It's amusing to me at times when people accuse me of racism. Most of my listeners have probably figured out that I am not a racist. In fact, I know that I have many black listeners and others of various races. My radio program appeals to people of all races and persuasions. And I am glad.

More importantly, as a Libertarian, I believe that laws should not be so specific that they enumerate "black" or "white," "man" or "woman." All people should, in an ideal world, be treated equally in the eyes of the law and in terms of their own individual responsibility for their actions. Unfortunately, I believe that racism still runs rampant in parts of this country and that when many people walk by someone on the street, they see first the color of their skin and not another person like themselves.

Another thing that this country supports, in an effort to be just, some say, is Affirmative Action quotas, wherein certain numbers of blacks have to be hired, certain numbers of Mexicans, and so on. This reeks of liberalism, handing out prizes as much as to say, here dog, jump for your bone, and it doesn't address the root problem: how people treat each other. In other words, just creating laws and regulations is not the solution to the basic human problem.

Militias

On my radio program, I have brought to light another great danger for America: the militias. Because of the increased dissatisfaction with our government, there are growing numbers of people who are banding together as militias. They are taking their right to bear arms and turning it into hatred. I believe it is a magnified hatred and paranoia of the government. Then there is the ATF and some segments of the FBI that are the antithesis of this militia movement. They are paranoid and hate the militias and I believe they are rushing at each other like two freight trains on the same track heading for an awful collision. I believe the bombing of the Oklahoma federal building was retaliation by militia members against the ATF and the FBI for their raid on the Branch Davidians in Waco, Texas. The Davidians of course were a peculiar brand of militia members held up in their compound with all sorts of artillery, waiting for Armageddon to occur.

People are losing faith in our government and our institutions. I remember as a youngster that every time the FBI announced the capture of a dangerous criminal, this instilled great respect for the FBI. Their word was as good as gold. It is not any longer. Now, the FBI is mistrusted, and even despised by many people in this country. I don't feel that our rights have disintegrated to such an extent that we have to grab a gun and take over the government. If you study history, you'll discover that most revolutions did not work; they were betrayed before they could. What is unique about the American Constitution is that it is structured in such a way that allows for change without the use of a gun, or of blowing up buildings, or subways, or poisoning people, or terrorizing people. Somehow there are those who have lost track of the way the Constitution is to work to our benefit.

Generally I would say that the militia issue did rear its head at Oklahoma City, but that our present threat is largely from biological weapons rather than people planting bombs. We had a large scare in Las Vegas with anthrax, and recent headlines in Britain showed them braced for a possible anthrax attack from Iraq. The ease with which people can access biological and chemical weapons has increased and consequently, so has the threat.

Overall, I worry about America. It appears that if we are not completely ruined because of an economic collapse, then it will be a social collapse, or a military confrontation that will damage this country. We are not what we once were.

And in the end. . .

It should be obvious by now that I am a complex, tangled mixture of a person who has had a myriad of life experiences that have shaped me into who I am today. I have settled into a personality and a lifestyle that makes me comfortable and happy. As you continue to read, you will get an even clearer picture of how the aspects of my personal life fit into the life I lead on the radio.

5

TRAVEL

I have done a great deal of traveling over the years, all over the world. It was my love for radio, and HAM radio in particular, which first made me curious about travel. I wanted to see the places of the people I talked to on my HAM radio. As a result, I developed travel lust. As a boy, I began traveling in my numerous attempts to run away from home. Then, the moment I could get away from home by enlisting in the Air Force, I almost immediately experienced worldwide travel. I traveled and lived in the Orient for years.

As a radio personality, I have had many opportunities to travel as part of my job. I have gone on cruises in the Caribbean, to South America, and to the Panama Canal. I have flown on the Concord from America to Paris, France and back. I actually had an opportunity to go up into the Concord cockpit doing MACH II, twice the speed of sound. I have since returned to the Orient, to Hong Kong, Tokyo, and Bangkok, Thailand to take a first hand look at those areas and report back to my listeners things of interest.

Overseas Travel

Flying overseas is just as challenging as you might imagine. No matter how long you have to prepare yourself for the fact that you are going to be suspended in a metal tube in the air for 10 plus hours, it is still tiring. And when you finally get to where you're going, you have this surreal feeling of being in a different country. No matter how much I travel, it is still hard to believe that in just a short time, you can go from the US to a completely different world. Americans stick out like sore thumbs in foreign countries, whether from reputation or just plain appearance.

How Lucky We Are

In my travels of the world, I have seen nearly everything representative of human existence. I have seen the abject poverty of hillside shanties in Thailand, to the riches of Tokyo and Hong Kong with their unbelievably limited space, a way of living I would never want to do, although I love the Japanese and their culture. Many Americans have no idea how good a place America is to live compared to other countries in the world. America is made up of a diverse, entrepreneurial, independent, thinking people. We are the most energetic, freedom loving, proud and argumentative people in the world.

Nowhere else in the world do people enjoy the freedom which I think we often take for granted. For example, in Thailand, you can go to jail just for criticizing the king. In Paris, they have clean streets and there is hardly any crime, but hardly anyone can afford the taxes to live there comfortably; they have their big socialist system controlling everything. In South America, they have instability, and you can't tell one day to the next what government you might have. In England, if the government orders you not to broadcast something, you cannot do it. You do not exactly have freedom of speech in that country.

We are spoiled in this country. We may complain of the justice system, but in most countries around the world, you have the burden of having to prove you are innocent of the crime you are accused of. And if you cannot, you rot in jail. At least in this country, as sluggish as the system may seem at times, you are given an opportunity to maintain your innocence until proven guilty. We have rights, privileges, and freedoms that we should cherish. While I was visiting communist China, I asked my tour guide if Chinese people are allowed to own guns. As I expected, he informed me that they are not allowed to own guns. I then told him that I not only own guns, but I possess my own Chinese AK-47 automatic rifle. His jaw practically dropped to the pavement.

One of the problems in this country is that the latest generations, including the Baby Boomers, Generation X, and the Baby Busters, are beginning to take the freedoms and privileges we have in this country for granted. They embrace the Bill of Rights, but they are not even thinking of assuming the bill of responsibilities. If our government made available round trip tickets to young people to visit a country of their choice, let them go there and make a study of that country and then return to America, they could see what they were missing when they left this country. It would be such an education; I don't think this country would be in half the trouble we're in right now if we would do that. People would come back from abroad and think how lucky they were to live here. Travel can put lots of things into perspective.

Reality Check

My wife and I, and a number of other people, visited the Orient together. I'm somewhat of an adventurous type, so while we were visiting Bangkok, I thought it would be interesting to visit the infamous world center for sex: Patpong. Patpong is basically just a street consisting of bars. Down in the middle of the street, there are street vendors selling T-shirts and other tourist-like commodities. In each bar, on either side of the street, there are girls willing to perform any type of sex for money. Nothing is illegal in Bangkok, including the exploitation of young children.

One of our most revolting discoveries came with finding young girls, maybe ten or twelve years old, dressing in American girl scout uniforms and making themselves available. We entered one of the bars briefly. There was a nude show going on, and there were young girls, perhaps 15, 16 or so years old, that would go around and hustle the customers. Eventually, we were approached by a beautiful Thai girl. who casually asked, "Do you have children?"

"No, we don't," my wife responded.

"Then, could I have one for you?" this girl said directly.

My wife decided that this was a little too forward and assumed her pretend Thai voice, "We go now," she said, looking sternly at me.

As bad as things are getting in America, at least we have not become so depraved that we allow very young girls to legally sell themselves. In America, we still have the remnants of the moral society that built this country. And I say this, even though I live in a state where prostitution is legal.

Europe Trip

A few years ago, I decided to travel to Russia and a few European countries. My focus was on Russia, of course, but Europe is filled with so much history that it made it an easy decision. Not only that, but also a great deal of what is happening in the world today is centered in Europe.

Russia

Besides the fact that Russia has had a formidable presence in the minds of most Americans in terms of that country's threat to us during the Cold War, I have always had a fascination with that part of the world. Russia has undergone quite a bit of social and cultural change recently and the country I saw was not the same country of which nuclear nightmares were conjured in our imaginations in the early 1980s.

We docked at St. Petersburg, on the Baltic Sea. Walking is usually the best way to see any city and we did plenty of that here. From St. Petersburg, we took a plane to Moscow. And not just any plane! We waited in line below the plane and consequently were able to see the plane's tires, filled with holes. Aeroflot is not your major maintenance airline. Their jets require brute power to keep flying; without it the plane is like a rock. The pilot flies like a robot and the bathroom was so bad your feet stuck to the floor.

You know how seats are supposed to lock in place? Well, Ramona was having a good time and she slapped the seat in front of her, the back of it, and two or three people went down like dominoes in front of her. In other words the seat has no locking mechanism at all. It just goes forward, you know, folds all the way forward. So she slapped this poor person and you can imagine how well that was received.

Moscow is a city spreading its wings. That's the best way I can describe it. Moscow has always been a symbol of Russia's spiritual and political power, so it's not surprising that the changes that are sweeping the country are clearly visible here. Where once there were state department stores, I saw these haphazard-looking street markets. Now as far as the people of Russia are concerned, there is more of a split than westerners might like to imagine. Take this example.

Russia has directorate offices for its various branches of what we think of as government. While we were in Moscow, we went privately to visit the Director of Communications and in his office he had a bust up on the wall. I said, "oh, that's Boris Yeltsin." And he started frowning. I looked again. Oops. It was Lenin. As far as he was concerned Boris Yeltsin could dry up and die. He's still a Communist. Not satisfied with leaving the obviously touchy subject alone and curious anyway, I said, "what do you think of Boris Yeltsin's new openness?" There's this crashing silence.

That's because it's still Communist. A lot of them miss what they had. They miss the old 'mother take care of all' structure.

Arriving in the Kremlin area, we walked through Red Square and sat by the Moscow River. This is the literal heart of Moscow. From here, you can travel in any direction and be overwhelmed by a vast array of monasteries, museums and buildings with breathtaking architecture. The churches with gold onion shaped tops were familiar to us from movies and CNN and were in profusion everywhere in Russia. In fact, that is one of the amazing things about the places we saw in Russia: everything was on such a large and grand scale.

We had lunch in the Kremlin so I did eat native food while I was there. I probably shouldn't have. Usually you don't even know what it is. They can't tell you, 'oh, famous Russian dish, you like.' It was goulash kind of stuff, salads and so on. It was a four or five course meal. The people who would serve the food came marching out, like with military music, and there was a band playing. It was really formal and I was really uncomfortable. I would say it's the equivalent of going to eat in the White House.

One of the highlights of Moscow was my visit to the Kremlin Armory. This is astounding; it's where all the billions of dollars in crown jewels are housed. I saw entire horse buggies made of diamonds and rubies. Unbelievable. If they were to sell that they would all be rich, but they won't because they're a very proud people. And this was a highlight of the trip also because it was when I almost got thrown in jail. Why? For filming the crown jewels of course. This big old Russian woman—I mean, just stereotypical, looked like a muscle lady with a Russian uniform— came up to me and almost slammed me to the floor. They're real serious there. You think Russia is this new open place——bullshit. You're watched every second. Of course we were there in the seat of power, too.

That's not all. On the tour, they have a Russian official who came along and watched, listened and monitored the tour guide. Going into Russia or Communist China is a really freaky

114

experience. It's actually scary. While we were in Red Square and we heard this bang and at the time nobody thought much about it. Later we found out that it was a bomb that had gone off. They had tried to assassinate Yeltsin while we were standing there. We couldn't go out at night there. It's very dangerous. They would kill you for your passport there very quickly. I'm glad I went and I don't think I will need to go again.

Every trip has its funniest moment and for me it happened on board the ship. One night they had a Russian theme night and the ship's officers dressed up as Russian officers. And I had little Art with me at the time. He was having himself a blast. He had at least six girls his age he had found on the ship and they were traipsing all over the place on the ship, places where they shouldn't be, like the casino. So here come these male and female officers. I said, "listen, if you see this 15-year old boy running around with a bunch of girls, why don't you stop him and arrest him." So they agreed.

Sure as hell, here comes this troop of six girls and Art. The officers said in Russian accents, "Are you Art Bell? Come with us now." He's freaking out he was so scared. They took him back to a little corner and started asking him all these questions. "Is it true that you were with six females? We were told this and we have observed it." And he says yes. So they started cracking up and they said "congratulations." Next Art comes up to my room and stomps as hard as he can on my foot. I said, "what the hell was that for?" He said, "for having me arrested!"

Although there is fast paced change taking place in many areas of Russia, you still cannot overlook the nearly 40 million people hovering below the poverty line and struggling to have some kind of decent life there. Despite the seemingly dark and gloomy nature of some parts of Russia, overall it was a fascinating adventure and full of discovery.

Norway

After Russia, we traveled to Oslo, Norway. What a difference a few hundred miles can make! This was one of the friendliest countries I have ever traveled to and Oslo was an amazing place. The people were gregarious and open to tourists, and the city was very clean.

When I was there, they were in the midst of a balmy blast of beautiful weather. In fact the Norwegians I talked to could not remember having such warm weather before. One of the best things about Europe in general is the unusual architecture. Norway is known for its stave churches, many of which are among the oldest wooden buildings in history, going all the way back to the Viking and early Christian time period.

I saw tons of castles in Oslo because there are castles everywhere. Filled with dungeons and dark cubbyholes, they are contrasted by the upper levels of banquet halls and staterooms, just like in your most vivid imaginations. They used light and dark woods of all types, crystal chandeliers, tapestries, and paintings, and through it all the cool chill of a stone and wood building. What gave me an even bigger chill was to walk through Akershus Castle, a medieval fortress and castle built around 1300. During World War II, the Nazis saw fit to use Akershus as a prison and execution center. I saw it as the center of lush park grounds and a picturesque location for views of the city and harbor.

I would really like to go back to Oslo one day. I was impressed by the tidiness of the city, by the contrasts between bustling activity and quiet oases of privacy and by the overall breathtaking landscape of the surrounding area.

Sweden

My next stop was Stockholm, Sweden. The mood in Stockholm was cheerful and upbeat, both because of the warm weather, and the fact that they were in the midst of celebrating their summer festival. Here I stayed within the confines of the city, but started on the top of the city, literally, looking over the tops of spiky cathedral roofs, and worked my way down to street level. Sweden struck me as a country of simple joys and that was truly appealing. Surrounded by fresh air, beautiful forests and huge lakes far off in the distance and the welcoming people, it was easy to relax even though we only had one day in port.

Europe Trip Overall

Overall, seeing Russia and Europe was unique from the standpoint that someone like myself, who watches the events that take place in those areas of the world every day on CNN, could finally 'put a face with a name,' so to speak. Europe and Russia have long histories, much longer than that of America, and the combination of seeing countries whose pasts are so tied up in their present was edifying. The trip put a lot of things into perspective because no matter how many books you read or television you watch, there is nothing that can replace actually being in a place and getting a feeling for what it is really about.

Mediterranean Cruise

It was with visions of pyramids dancing in my head that I planned my cruise through the center of ancient civilization. I was also attracted by thoughts of clean white stucco buildings in the Mediterranean and the Holy Land of Jerusalem was shrouded in mystery and intrigue for me. So I had plenty of reasons to travel to places where the contrasts would range from hot and dusty to cool and breezy.

Athens, Greece

When we arrived in Athens, we were exhausted. The Athens airport, not a huge, bustling airport as you might think in a city that size, was sheer chaos. After we passed through customs (comprised of four looooong lines), the next challenge was getting our luggage off the carousels. There was no way to tell where you could get your flight's luggage and there were four or five different carousels. So everyone was running everywhere.

Getting to the hotel was a journey through a maze of narrow streets, packed with every size of vehicle in existence: buses, small

European cars and, most of all, scooters. Fearlessly, people rode (without helmets) through traffic that made Los Angeles look like a Sunday drive, zipping in and out, not hesitating to challenge heavy chunks of metal (also known as buses) twenty times their size. The cab drivers were imbued with a similar sense of confidence in their driving skills, veering in and out of traffic casually. I finally decided just not to look, or I would lose my mind, although I have no problem with speed.

Once we got past the initial stage of exhaustion, we were ready for fun. In Athens for a few days before we were scheduled to sail, we went to see the Acropolis. In the United States, the price of marble is often through the ceiling. But as we walked up the long, winding path to the Acropolis, slabs of raw marble lay everywhere, untouched, polished only by people's shoes walking on them. It was unbelievable that something that is considered so valuable in this country could just be laying around in Greece!

The Acropolis is situated, as you know, on the top of a large hill. Surrounding these ruins is the city of Athens in all directions. From where we stood, the city was smoggy and packed with buildings. The Acropolis itself is a wondrous thing. No matter how many pictures you look at, you cannot replace the real thing. Currently Athenian officials are attempting to restore much of the original building, as it has been gradually falling apart due to wind and weather. I reflected upon the building: how many historical figures had walked through it, how it was constructed—another mind-boggling thing especially when I saw how huge these columns and pieces of marble were.

At the hotel, our room was on the tenth floor, so Bob Crane and I thought it would be the perfect time to test the satellite phone we had with us. The whole group of us, the Cranes, Ramona and my publisher and editor, who were also on the trip, was standing on the balcony of my hotel room while we called Alan Corbeth in Oregon. The connection was great, with only a little bit of delay. How strange it was to talk to someone literally a world apart and feel as if they were right next door.

Feeling the giddiness of our trip, we also launched several paper airplanes from the balcony, as well as some lilies from the bouquet of flowers in our room. People below must have thought we were crazy or having a party because here are these flying objects coming down on them. One of my airplanes actually lodged itself in the side view mirror of a parked car, which we all cheered as an unusual landing.

The Ship

If you are someone who has not done a lot of traveling, or even if you have and you want a unique way of seeing many places in a short amount of time, I highly recommend a cruise. Being aboard a ship means you only unpack once. Holland America Line holds a particularly special place in my heart because of how attentive their staff is to your every need. This ship line employs Philippino staff and you will be hard pressed to find a more polite, friendly people.

Our ship board experience began with a fire drill for the entire ship, actually standard procedure for most cruise lines. After all, if something happens at sea, you better know where the lifeboat you are in is located unless you feel like swimming. So we went through that, complete with bulky orange life jackets, all of which was conducted with the utmost of seriousness by the ship's Scandinavian officers.

The ship we were on, the MS Maasdam (pronounced "Mahz-dahm") was like a floating palace. It was huge, 700 plus feet from end to end, and filled with art treasures and pieces of sculpture collected from its various travels around the world. There are about twelve levels on the ship, most of which are passenger berths, or suites. The upper levels contain things like pools, observation decks, an exercise facility, various bars and restaurant areas and general gathering places. Another nice thing about Holland America Lines is that they usually have about 1200 people on board the ship during any cruise, which results in many opportunities for privacy and relaxation.

When I travel, I tend to bring my favorite technology with me, like my Sangean radio, my binoculars, etc. This was particularly important for the cruise since even though there were phones on the ship, the cost for using them was so prohibitive that you might as well not have had them. We also got a real blast out of using the satellite phone on board the ship, and even called the network in Oregon to report in on what we were doing, which they then passed on to my listeners. Of course, the room was also equipped with a television on which movies played, but more importantly, the position of the ship and the conditions at sea were constantly displayed.

During the month of October, when we cruised, the weather was just about perfect. Temperatures were in the 70s and the sun was deceptively strong; conditions were, in a word, idyllic. Most people who have sailed on boats know that you experience rocking, but it is much different on a ship this size. Equipped with stabilizers, we had about as smooth a ride as if we were floating through the air (with one exception, which I will go into later). When we were at open sea, there was no land in sight, nothing but the gentle swells of the crystal blue water below us, and the clear blue sky above.

Cairo, Egypt

In my mind, I always imagined that I would someday go to the pyramids in Cairo, Egypt. Arriving at the port of Alexandria, Egypt, we were driven the three hours to Cairo in a private bulletproof car. We had contacted the Director of Antiquities, Zahi Hawass, ahead of time to assure that we would be banned from absolutely nothing, and rode in the car with him. The cities of Cairo and Giza are characterized by drifting sand, searing blue skies and people wrapped in layers of cloth—inordinately heavy for the heat.

Outside of the pyramids, I was given a demonstration of how the blocks were made for the pyramids. A group of us gathered around this one fellow with a sledgehammer and a large rock of limestone. I was very skeptical; I didn't think he could ever break that rock! Of course he did break it, exactly in half. The director said, "See Art, this is how the pyramids were built." Everyone wonders how the pyramids were constructed and to have such a simple demonstration in front of my eyes was mind-blowing.

The entrance to the Great Pyramid is a stone tunnel basically carved into the side of the pyramid. The tunnel then veers sharply upward with about a 4-foot high clearance for 180 feet. You have to stoop over to get up and people are coming up and going down the same way because there is no other exit or entrance. I know now that I will be living a few more years because if I were going to have a heart attack from exertion I would have had it going up the pyramid. After the first tunnel, there was another path that went sharply and vertically toward the sky, then more ducking under stone.

At the top of this excruciating climb, we came to an empty stone room that was in fact at the top of the pyramid. This was called the King's Chamber and contained an empty, broken sarcophagus. I jumped right into the sarcophagus and experienced an extremely strange vibration in resonance to your voice when you lie inside what is essentially a stone tomb. It was somewhat eerie being inside a place where once a mummy had been!

One of the highlights in Egypt was when Ramona and I were taken to an area that has been excavated for the last year in Giza. There were hundreds of graves. According to the Director, this was the burial ground for the people who built the pyramids. How do we know this? The Director informed me that it was because there were beautiful hieroglyphics showing how the pyramids were built and the various jobs they did. I was told not to take pictures, but had already snapped a few.

One of the more "tourist-y" things you can do in Cairo (besides the pyramids) is to ride a camel. So of course we did that! I got bravely on to the back of one creature that was covered in brightly colored blankets and tassels, and leaned back, so I wouldn't fall off. With a dangerous swaying motion, this humped animal climbed to its feet and the ground fell away below me. We picked a slow trail through an old cemetery filled with stone grave markers and over to a view of all three of the Giza pyramids. The ride lasted only ten minutes, but I was unexpectedly and ruefully sore immediately afterwards.

Israel

Our arrival at Haifa, Israel was shrouded in tense drama, as Israeli secret service had to clear the ship before anyone could go ashore. Uniformed Israeli men and women, looking not the slightest bit humorous, sifted through passports from everyone on the ship, setting aside those who they actually wanted to have a look at in person.

South of where the Maasdam docked, behind a bizarre series of gates and barbed wire fencing lies one of Israel's more important industries: the refining of cut diamonds. We visited the so-called diamond factory where we viewed the four 'Cs' of diamonds: color, clarity, cut, carat. What a fascinating thing, to see what a raw diamond looks like (pretty unimpressive) and see what the tooling delivered afterward (amazing, as any woman will tell you). Upstairs, after the small tour of the tooling area, we were greeted with a large showroom filled with diamonds and various other stones.

Docking at Ashdod, I traveled to Jerusalem by cab. Along the way, I saw fields of cotton that grew right up to the road and even drove through vast expanses of green which, our driver informed us, were *kibbutz*. A *kibbutz* is basically a common upon which Israelis volunteer to work and support agriculture for the good of the nation. What a thing to think about, especially living in a country like America where it is all for one and forget anyone else!

Jerusalem looks like a mass of smallish stone buildings that spread over the rolling hills in neatly packed lines. All of the buildings in the city are built using stone that has been quarried from Jerusalem; any construction that takes place must use this stone and no other.

Arriving in the Holy Places, I saw various stone walls rising in various directions, and passed through security checkpoints and metal detectors all along the way to our first stop: the Wailing Wall. The Wailing Wall is the last wall that remains of what the Jews believe is the temple. Men and women are separated into two sides as they approach the wall and women cover their heads as they go to leave prayers on paper or to pray aloud.

Adjacent to the Wailing Wall is the synagogue where no women are allowed inside. I walked in and along the walls made of wood, I saw men dressed in black with *yarmulke*, muttering over what looked like the torah. The whole experience was somewhat strange. The places refuse to be a tourist attraction, although they are; instead I was left with this eerie, solemn feeling, as if I were trampling over something sacred.

The Holy City is divided into quarters; for instance, there is the Jewish quarter, the Arab quarter and so on. What this entails is different areas where Jews and Arabs have restaurants and open shops. Walking through the Arab quarter, you would see shops with fabrics of dark fuschia and purple for sale, beads, etc.

Everywhere in the Holy City, I saw children with guns. In fact, guns were prevalent all over my stops in Israel. Even standing in line at the ATM, the Israeli man in front of me had a large caliber weapon shoved into his belt. All Israelis are required to serve in the army; thus, dozens of what looked to me to be teenagers walked in uniform with AK-47s slung over their shoulders as casually as we carry backpacks here in America.

In Bethlehem, we traveled to the exact place where Christ was believed to be born, and then went to Jerusalem and saw the exact place where Christ died. I had a very strong reaction to all of this; it's impossible *not* to have a strong reaction. I think most Americans are like me, and are not Sunday churchgoers. All your life in Sunday school (I went to Sunday school) you're told about the birth of Christ and his life and his death. But to actually go there and see the spot where that occurred is really sobering. You realize, my god, here it is, it's real, it's not the old days of Sunday school, here it is. That causes you to step back a little bit and go, whoa!

Greek Islands

After the intense nature of the first part of our cruise through the Middle East, it was almost a relief to head for the Greek islands. This was particularly true when it came to the heat and dryness of the climates in both the Middle East and Egypt.

We arrived at an area of Rhodes called "Old Town." Like the rook piece in chess, there was a long, stone wall surrounding an area of open front shops. Even the city was protected by a breakwater, firing the imagination into reliving battles of days gone by. In many places, the streets were made of stone, individually laid in place, and Rhodes was filled with cats, which we loved. Cats are a common thing on the Greek islands, but Rhodes cats seemed to possess an independent, sparkly personality all their own. Content to mildly observe nearby tourists or to race around on the tops of stucco walls, they were a pleasure to see and photograph.

Rhodes also presented us with the first opportunity to see nude beaches, again a common thing on many Greek islands. Although the beaches were right next to the road in many cases and were pebbly instead of sandy in places, people flocked to them, clothes or no clothes. We also encountered a beautiful woman on Rhodes, who looked as clean and pure as the Mediterranean Sea itself.

Standing on its own rocky peninsula with a foreboding stone fort at the top, Nafplion is the epitome of a relaxed Greek island. Men sat idly sipping coffee and toying with worry beads. We felt a genuine hospitality; the shopkeepers whose stores we frequented were friendly, sometimes offering us a cold beer even if we were just looking. I was struck at the difference between American and European attitudes in this regard. Americans are much more likely to want to come into a shop and look, to be left alone. Europeans view visitors in their shops much like visitors in their homes, and are accordingly gracious most of the time.

The intriguing attraction of Nafplion is definitely the 1,000 steps built into a mountain and leading to a castle-like structure at the top. In 1822, after the beginning of the Greek War of Independence, the Greeks took this hilltop fortress from the Turks. Besides its obvious defensive purpose and place in history, the appearance of this many steps was dizzying. Made of stone and frequently with no side railings, these were not for the faint of heart—or body. Which was why I stayed away from them! Bob and Sue Crane plodded bravely up them and returned later, red-faced and sweating, while Ramona and I sat in the shade of the olive and eucalyptus trees and drank quart bottles of Heineken.

Volcano Sighting

The last day at sea was a Sunday, and we were all jammed to capacity with all the sights and sounds of the last two weeks. We were due to arrive in Naples, Italy the next morning and so anticipated relaxing and recovering from our Greek Islands experiences of the last four days. It was not to be so. Around mid-day, the ship began to rock more and more steadily. Now, as I have told you, the stabilizers erased virtually all motion from the Maasdam, but this kind of motion was beyond control. By early evening, the decks had cleared of people and the winds had begun whipping the ship with up to sixty mile per hour gale force. The swells reached between eighteen and twenty-seven feet.

As it was the last day that our little group would be together, and we knew that we would be passing an active volcano in the Strait of Messina, we gathered in one of the suites and ate a light dinner. We believed, as per the television monitor in the room, that we would be passing the volcano on the port side, which was why we were gathered in this particular suite. As the clock hit 7pm, we noticed with some dismay that we were apparently passing the volcano on the starboard side. Hurriedly, we rushed over to my suite; my editor and I reached the balcony first, and both of us yelled against the wind, "Oh my god!"

There in front of us, towering over the ship, was the volcano (named Stromboli), spewing orange lava straight into the air. It was breathtaking. It was amazing. No one among us had seen an active volcano before that night, and despite the powerful winds screaming into our faces, we stood awestruck on the balcony watching the volcano until we sailed out of sight. I even used my night vision scope and was able to see the lava in the air above the volcano!

Riding the adrenaline of the volcano sighting, we trooped up to the observation deck at the top of the ship. There the real strength of the winds was truly evident. Flags flapping in a persistent beating pattern, but we heeded no physical signs that we should be tucked away in our rooms. It was crazy, but when else in your life could you experience something like this? Suddenly, I felt the wind sneak under my glasses and the next thing I knew, it whipped them off my face! Well, I didn't expect to see those glasses again, but after everyone crawled around on the deck looking, Bob Crane found them right next to the railing. I consider that a minor miracle.

By this time, some people in our party (who shall remain nameless) were starting to look a little green from all the rocking of the ship (and I mean this thing was *really* rocking—you couldn't even walk down a hallway in a straight line). So we disbanded to our rooms, but let me assure you, it was no easy task getting to sleep that night. First of all, the surface you are standing on is moving. Then you get into bed and are lying horizontally on a moving surface; it was bizarre and a bit unsettling. There were some bad moments during that night when the ship hit waves head on, or at least it felt like that, and we began to wonder how safe we really were.

We can laugh about it now, but then we were reflecting on our position: in open sea with no land for miles, pitch black night—it was enough to make most people start praying. Anyway, they must have been doing something like that considering the whole ship was holed up in their rooms!

126

Naples & Rome, Italy

Arriving in Naples, we were greeted by the shadowy visage of Mount Vesuvius, its looming presence promising to emerge from the early morning fog. We were worn out by the nearly two weeks of intensive travel, but we were determined to see Pompeii, the buried, ashen city. And indeed we did. What a bizarre feeling to know that there were humans buried under all that ash.

Naples itself was interesting because of all the colors on the buildings. The stone and stucco was mustard yellow, faded red and sometimes even a sky blue. I walked through alleyways that were miniature cities in and of themselves: people hanging clothing from windows, shouting across the sky to each other, open air markets in the dark gloom of the tall buildings that overshadowed it all.

In Rome, we were in Vatican City, when a clamor arose and there in front of me was the Pope. Talk about a case of being in the right place at the right time! I also went to the Vatican, and walked partway up a long, winding staircase that was one of the more striking features of the building.

Mediterranean Cruise Overall

Overall, the Mediterranean trip was nothing short of incredible. If I had to pick a high point it would probably be when I was in the Giza area, looking at all the astounding pyramids. With all the new discoveries being made about Egyptian history, this area held an especially strong allure for me.

Alaska

I have one word for Alaska: unforgettable. Imagine being right up against a glacier, and it's dead silent, and the water looks like a bluish mirror and there's ice floating in the water. Suddenly you'll hear something that sounds like a rifle crack, and a big piece of ice will break off right in front of you and fall into the water. Of course, that is probably the main attraction, the glaciers. From the mammoth Columbia Glacier in Prince William Sound to the Hubbard Glacier in Yakutat Bay, I was in awe of this silent, beautiful land.

A feeling of wildness and of an untamed nature pervaded me as I stared at the gleaming white mountains leaping into the air around me, and viewed such abundant wildlife as sea otters, caribou, polar bears, moose, and grizzly bears. We were pleasantly surprised to find that it was not really cold, but at night it did get to be a little cold, say, light jacket weather. The best time to go is in the fall and we were there in August 1997, which was pretty close to perfect.

I was especially lucky on this trip and got to see a Blackhawk helicopter and even sit in it! With my fascination for flying, this was a dream come true. We also visited an old nighttime friend, Charles Gray, a former engineer from KENI in Juneau, Alaska.

Overall, I felt proud that this land still existed in large part untouched in all its vast and majestic beauty. Not only has Alaska played an important part in history, with the gold rush, but it offers such varied climates that there is probably something there to appeal to everyone. Whether you want to be in a place where you can see the stars at night or hear the roar of a waterfall cascading over a hundred foot cliff, gape in amazement as huge glaciers drift past or experience the culture of the area (Russian dancers at Sitka), Alaska is definitely an adventure I would recommend to anyone. Although I saw Alaska via a cruise ship, I would also like to go back someday and see the interior of Alaska by train. I have heard this is an absolutely breathtaking way to visit this land that already enthralls me just by what I have seen of it.

Australia, Africa & Beyond

I was once actually offered a job in Perth, Australia. Because of the exchange rates, at the time anyway, you would live pretty well in Australia, but you would never be able to save enough money to ever return to the United States again. So I decided against that.

*My mother, Jane Gumaer
publicity photo, 1943.*

*My dad, Arthur W. Bell II
Guadalcanal
publicity photo, 1942.*

My parents the newlyweds in a garden photo, August 26, 1944.

First house I lived in, New River, North Carolina.

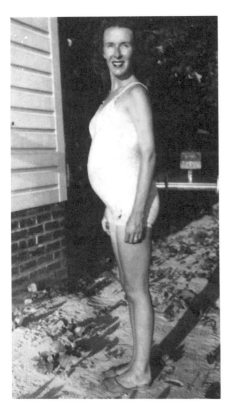

My mom is pregnant with me. The night before at the officer's club, they threatened to follow her around with a basket. In the next photo, that's pretty much where I end up.

I'm one month old here sleeping happily in my mom's laundry basket, 1945.

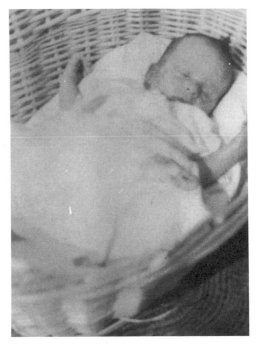

That's me with two stuffed friends, August 6, 1945.

A great picture of my mom and I when I was two or three.

My sisters Jesse, Tina and I with an equine friend.

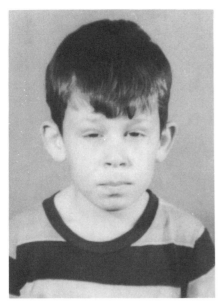

*First day of kindergarten , 1951.
I was not particularly thrilled.*

*12 years old in my Cub Scout
uniform and I already have my
cheesy grin.*

*In all my glory on the top floor of the Blue Ridge Summit house
surrounded by what I love. 13 years old.*

The house in Blue Ridge Summit.

16, smoking and ready to see the world, 1961.

Looking very serious in my Air Force uniform, 1963.

Paul Gerrard, Lynn Witlake and me celebrating our radio freedom at KMED.

A young, but enthusiastic radio fanatic, I am in front of the KMED studio equipment.

KSBK TOP 30

... Call For Your Favorite Daily At 883-4530
Or Write To KSBK C P O Box 4, Naha, Okinawa

Vol. 4 No. 45   November 18, 1967

There I am, looking much more energetic than I did 155 hours later with the world record in my pocket.

KDON Castroville, California 30 years old.

Taking a Vietnamese orphan to safety, 1975.

Tinkering with the cable headend system I helped build at Times-Mirror.

My studio at home, launching pad for Coast to Coast and Dreamland.

My cats, Shadow, Comet and Abby.

Claire Reese helped me get started in night talk radio at KDWN, Las Vegas.

Ramona and a friend in Norway.

My beautiful soulmate and I.

Alleged ghost as photographed by stone mason.

Hale-Bopp comet.

My boss and friend Alan Corbeth

Talkers Award Ceremony

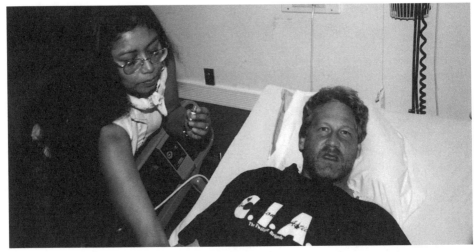

Ramona visits Dannion Brinkley in hospital after his third brush with death.

*My Egyptian friend
Zahi Hawass.*

*Whitley Strieber
visited me*

*Ramona and I flanked
on either side by
Bob & Sue Crane (left),
Jennifer Osborn &
Werner Riefling (right)
on the Egypt cruise.*

I'm posing with the Alaska Air Guard and a Blackhawk helicopter.

I signed hundreds of copies of my book "The Quickening" at the San Diego booksigning.

But I remain fascinated with the area and have contemplated a trip there.

I think that for my next trip I would like to see Africa. I would do it by balloon safari because that way I could see the animals and not disturb them. And of course I am fascinated by the idea of seeing the Nile River.

For me, traveling is a good way to realize how much I appreciate living in America, for one thing. It is also interesting to me to see how the other cultures live, and I feel that the knowledge and exposure I gain from traveling affects the way I look at what happens in the country I live in. Finally, traveling makes me glad that I have a place as private as my home is. I can venture out, see what I want to see, and reflect upon it in the quiet and serenity of my own space. Like they say, it's always good to get home.

6

MY START IN RADIO

It was during my stint with the armed services that I inadvertently began my radio career. I was stationed at Amarillo Air Force Base at the time. Normally, on a military base, radios are used for communications with other bases, aircraft, or various military personnel for official military purposes. Generally, an area on a base is dedicated to handling radio dispatches. Access to radio equipment, particularly HAM type radio equipment, was very easy. Anyway, I was aware of this, and tucked this away in my mind.

One day I was bored and I missed using my HAM radio, which had been my passion for many years, right up until I enlisted in the Air Force. Just for the hell of it, I started poking around the base to see what I could find. I eventually secured for myself a Heathkit Variable Frequency Oscillator (VFO). The Heathkit VFO was used essentially to drive a HAM radio transmitter. With my knowledge and skill in electronics, I was able to convert this VFO to operate on the AM band. Then, in my barracks room, I figured a way to put music to this VFO and it managed to transmit to the barracks located around the base. Just for fun, I began transmitting music to the guys in the barracks. Most of the guys loved it. They just tuned in their radios and every night for quite some time they got music without commercial interruption.

Uh, Not In the Barracks, Guys

Eventually, our first sergeant found out about this, and he talked to the commanding officer. The commanding officer decided that he did not want us to have our own little radio station in the barracks. By this time, I had met Lynn Witlake (my friend with the passion for stormy weather), who became involved with my little enterprise, as well as Paul Gerrard, another good friend (eventually a police officer in New Jersey). Lynn and Paul were very much involved, and the commanding officer called us in to confront all of us about this radio station.

"What are you guys up to with this radio thing?" the commanding officer wanted to know.

"Well, we thought it would be okay to just play music to the guys on the base. So, we made a radio transmitter," I responded meekly.

The commanding officer pondered this for a moment. Then he looked at the three of us standing there at attention.

"You know, guys, you really shouldn't be doing this in the barracks," he said, somberly. "What I'm going to do is call the military amateur radio station commander on the base and see if they would be willing to give you a couple of rooms where you can do your broadcast."

Upon hearing this, our little eyes lit up, and we got all excited. I couldn't believe it, I thought we were going to get reprimanded, maybe end up cleaning toilets for the next week. And yet, the commanding officer all but told us to start our own radio station. We were surprised and elated. We all said, "Yes, yes, yes, let's do it!" And so we did.

Neither the commanding officer, nor anyone else for that matter, had any concept of commercial broadcasting, what was legal or illegal; they just wanted to get this situation handled. The barracks was not logical to them, but getting us over to the radio people seemed to make sense. So, right away, our commanding officer called the commanding officer of the radio station and made the necessary arrangements. And for whatever reason, the radio station commander said, "Absolutely, sounds good. Send them over. We can give your men a couple of rooms and anything else they need." And over we went.

With the commanding officer's blessings, we managed to build an entirely illegal, pirate radio station in this MARS building. MARS, incidentally, means Military Amateur Radio Service. In hindsight, this was obviously meant to be for me, for this began my radio career, although it began outside the law with an illegal radio station.

KMED Takes Flight

In the two rooms allotted us, we built a complete studio, equipped with record turntables, a board to control everything, a microphone, noisemakers, and all the other usual studio trappings. Since there were numerous telephone poles and long antennas available to us, and we had pretty much all the room we needed, I decided first to get a higher powered radio transmitter and convert this to the broadcast band. We also erected for ourselves a huge antenna, about 300 feet long. Then, we went on the air. When we first went on the air, you could not only hear us at the barracks, but all over Amarillo Air Force Base. All the barracks at all the facilities could hear us. We became an instant hit. Everyone loved our radio station, which we called Amarillo, KMED. These were call letters that were not assigned to us; we just made them up, based on the fact that the Air Force base was part of a medical squadron.

We had a marvelous time. After a while, we discovered that the transmitter and the antenna worked a little too well. Why? Because we were also picked up about 30 miles away by the city of Amarillo. At that time, the city of Amarillo had about 150,000 people. As we were not only on daily, but also on a 24-hour schedule, and we provided the popular music of the day without commercial interruption, this made it very difficult for the legitimate commercial stations to compete with us. But somehow, we managed to stay on the air without any hindrance for a full year.

Every once in a while, in the world of radio, a survey is conducted which is called an Arbitron survey. This is to determine how many people are listening to each radio station in a given geographic area. The radio stations are then ranked for the market they cover. Unfortunately for us, KMED showed up on this Arbitron survey. Every commercial radio station in the city of Amarillo went nuts. Not only did they realize we existed, but they also realized we were probably robbing them of a significant number of their audience. After all, we were playing the same music and were just as fun to listen to, all without commercials. Naturally, they wanted to get rid of us.

Complaints reached the commander of our base and once again we found ourselves in his office. This time he was not so supportive. In clear, strong terms, it was explained to us that we had an illegal radio station, what we were doing was illegal, and that KMED was history from that point forward. And that was that. Despite its short-lived history, KMED was significant to me as my entry into the world of professional broadcasting.

Entering the Real World

After my four-year stint with the Air Force, I returned home in 1966, and wanted to get into radio. Despite a brief technician job with ITT in New Jersey, in which my love of electronics and technical things was expounded, it seemed that nothing could prevent me from being pulled in the direction of radio.

To my good fortune, on the basis of my enthusiasm, my obvious knowledge of studio equipment, my HAM radio license, and my year of experience as a disc jockey (albeit at the illegal KMED), I managed to wiggle my way into my first professional broadcasting position at a religious radio station located on top of a mountain in Franklin, New Jersey. For purposes of confidentiality, I'll just call this station KREL. The location of KREL was fine in the summer, but in the winter, when it snowed, it was a treacherous trek to drive up the mountain to get to the station. Anyway, my first program consisted of reading the news, which I did between the religious programming. That's all I did.

Now the station manager had this eccentricity about broadcasters speaking too close to the microphone. He hated it when you could hear the "pff, pff," when a host spoke into the microphone, especially when pronouncing words with "P" in them. His way of correcting people who were in the habit of speaking too close to the microphone was to pull the chair out from under them. Apparently, he thought I had this habit, so every once in a while, he would sneak in and pull the chair right out from under me. Listeners heard a thud and a groan as I hit the floor. You can guess that I was quickly broken of this habit.

Return to the Orient

After working for KREL for a few months, I went to a radio station in a little town called Bath, New York. I worked there for about eight months. It was during this eight months in particular that I longed more than ever to go back to the Far East. But for the longest time, I could not figure out how to do it without re-enlisting in the Air Force. Eventually, I decided to write a letter to the only English speaking radio station in the Orient, KSBK, located in Naha, Okinawa, the capital city. KSBK was a Japanese-owned company which consisted of the radio station and a Japanese television station, but it was broadcasting the radio to about 250,000 Americans living on the island of Okinawa (mostly American military and their dependents). Along with the letter, I sent a tape of my work. I demonstrated how I could play and introduce music, how I could do the news, and so on.

One day, after anxious waiting, much to my amazement and delight, I received a letter informing me that my employment had been accepted. I would work on a contractual basis and I must agree to serve a minimum of a year in Okinawa, and I could start on such and so a day. They even arranged for my airfare and a flight out there, and guaranteed a flight back to the US when I was ready to return. I remember jumping up and down with excitement after reading the letter; I was going back to a place I loved.

This time returning to the Orient, I really had it made. I was not controlled by the military in any way. The Okinawa police gave me a little black book that was intended to record my activities, and they were at least theoretically in control of my activities on the island. Generally, however, the island police just assumed that as an American I was under control of the American military, so they left me alone. And the American military assumed I was under control of the island police. In fact, no one was in control of me, and I was *out* of control.

My time at KSBK was absolutely a wild time in my life. When I wasn't in the studio, we did live remote broadcasts, usually from the bar district. We would just set up with our equipment and talk to the people at some select bar. This was an advertisement for the bar, and it brought attention to our station. On the air, at these remote broadcasts, we would tell people what a fun place a particular bar was, and how the ladies were so good looking and so on. This was all meant to entice GIs into the bar, and it worked.

Breaking Records at KSBK

It was not long before I became a very popular disc jockey playing music, doing the news, and I even did a little talk radio. But apart from the daily routine of broadcasting and these occasional bar remotes, I also participated in breaking a couple of world records to draw attention to the station.

The first record I broke while at KSBK was a continuous broadcast record. I was on the air continuously for 115 hours and 15 minutes. I started on a Monday afternoon, and I kept at it, non-stop, until Saturday afternoon. Most of the time I played music, but I would talk a little between each selection. This broadcasting marathon got a lot of attention and many people dropped by the station to cheer me on. Probably half the island at some point tuned me in just to listen to the DJ who was doing the world record broadcast. I was even visited every so often by various doctors and nurses to check up on me to make sure I was all right. They would take my pulse, respiration, and blood pressure. At first I drank coffee, but after a while they wouldn't let me drink coffee because they worried about me. To stay awake, I would take cans of frozen tomato juice and orange juice and hold them against my carotid artery. Doing this actually shocked me awake.

This was an odd experience, mostly because of the sleep deprivation. After a few days without sleep, I became delirious and it was as though I entered a different world. There were a couple of times things got very strange for me. I knew I was awake, and I was walking around, and I didn't fall over or anything, but I distinctly remember that I was not in reality. I just lost touch with reality. This was a very disconcerting experience for me. Normally, I am in control and am very much aware of everything going on around me. But without sleep, my mind started to do some weird things. I felt as though I were floating around in a different world, opening refrigerators, walking up and down stairs, but not really feeling as though I were part of this world. It was frightening. But I did it, I broke the world record in endurance broadcasting. I would never do this again. Once in a lifetime is enough for me. Of course, not long after, a disc jockey in Denver broke the record. For me, however, this stunt did a great deal to increase my popularity at KSBK, although I am also convinced I incurred some permanent physical and possible mental damage as a result of this stupid stunt.

KSBK got a lot of publicity because of the world record broadcast. About a year later, I participated in another publicity effort. This time I would be part of a team to break the world seesawing record while broadcasting. To make it all the more interesting to the general public, we decided to stage this event as a contest. After soliciting for a partner on the air, I ended up with a Navy guy who must have been as or only slightly more crazy than I was. The rules were that we had to seesaw continuously. No stopping for breaks, for eating, for sleeping, even for going to the bathroom. No one could ever get off the seesaw. And then, as part of the contest, we challenged a pair of Marines. They got the days off they needed, and they got on another seesaw right next to us.

136

This spectacle was held out in the middle of the hot, tropical sun of Okinawa. At night everything was fine because there was no heat but the heat in the daytime made it very difficult to keep going. Nevertheless, we all relentlessly seesawed on. During most of this contest, many listeners turned out to see how we were proceeding. There was a great deal of enthusiasm and support. People would drive by and honk horns, or just cheer us on.

Apart from just staying awake and doing the broadcast from the seesaw, there were some other challenges. For one thing, how did we relieve ourselves? Fortunately, the need for going number two did not come up; otherwise, we would really have had a problem. But, there was a need to take care of number one. Well, someone very resourcefully came up with the idea of getting the relief bags used by fighter pilots. They strapped these bags to our legs with a tube going to the appropriate place on our anatomy and that's how we did it. Of course, there was the embarrassing part of someone having to come along to remove the bag and then replacing it while we were still seesawing, but it was better than not having the choice!

How did this thing end? And who won?

About 40 hours into the competition, one of the Marines finally passed out and fell off the seesaw. Poor guy. They literally carried him away on a stretcher in an ambulance. The second Marine was automatically disqualified, but he was about ready to pass out anyway and he gratefully went off into the sunset. This meant we beat them as far as that part of the competition was concerned. But we still needed to continue because we had a world record to break. We kept at it for another 17 hours for a total of an incredible 57 hours and a new world record. In the end, it got both Art Bell and KSBK a lot of good publicity. Ah, the things you do when you're young and stupid.

I was with KSBK for six years and my future in radio in Okinawa was promising. But as fate would have it, I found myself struggling with a very difficult situation in my personal life which made it practically impossible for me emotionally to remain at a job I loved in a part of the world I loved. As I explained earlier, the

Japanese woman I was living with at the time developed progressive mental illness, and despite all the efforts to help her, nothing worked. I stayed with her for several years, trying to help. Eventually, especially when she no longer even knew who I was, it became clear to me that the relationship was over. And somehow, it was simply too difficult for me to continue to live in the city where we met, fell in love, and lived together. I can only conclude that it must have been my destiny, cruel as it seemed at the time, to leave the Orient.

My Return to Rock

After KSBK, I continued my radio experience by returning to America. And I spent the better part of the next twenty years in rock music radio. Over the years, I have held positions as music director and news director; I have done morning shows, afternoon shows, and evening shows; I have done regular old rock and roll, top 40 rock, and on and on. If it was done in rock music during the 1960s and the 1970s, I probably did it. And I was very good at what I did. I was always one of the most popular rock radio DJs in any given radio market where I worked and consequently achieved the highest ratings. At this point, I couldn't do it anymore, and I wouldn't do it anymore. I would now find it boring and intellectually non-challenging, but at the time, I was young, it was the thing to do, and I was good at it.

Radio is a very volatile, insecure business. They say you are only as good as your last show. This may not be exactly true, but it is awfully close. During those twenty odd years, I moved and shifted from station to station. Moving around was part of the lifestyle of radio. I often refer to it as a gypsy lifestyle. The majority of my years in radio were spent on the West Coast, although I did a brief stint with stations in North Carolina and in Anchorage, Alaska. In the late 1970s, I even worked at a station in Connecticut, which of course is the area of the country where I more or less grew up.

This Connecticut station was WAVZ, in New Haven (by the way, one of my current affiliates and the station my mother listens to me on). WAVZ was a FM station, which was significant, as most rock music stations were AM. In fact, during the early days, particularly during the 1960s, the heyday of rock and roll, most of the radio stations that played rock music were AM stations. It was only years later that FM stations proclaimed they would take over the world of radio. I had just been hired by WAVZ and during the night before I was to do my first morning show at WAVZ, a great deal of snow had fallen.

Now, after my experience with tropical climates in the Orient, and my exposure to the drier climate of the West Coast, I became partial to warmer, sub-tropical weather. In Connecticut, however, it was usually cold, snowy weather in the winter, and muggy in the summer, an atmosphere which I just got weary of. So, there I was, just having passed my audition with flying colors, went through the rigmarole of becoming unionized for the job, and was supposed to start for work, to begin this new morning show. At least I started with good intentions that morning. Then I went outside to my car, which was buried under several feet of snow. Then, as if it weren't enough that I had to clear it of snow, it would not start. I just sat there and thought, "This sucks!" I didn't want to do it. I would not put up with this type of weather. I didn't even bother calling the radio station to let them know what was going on. I went right back into my apartment, packed my stuff into my car, and drove to Miami, Florida. I didn't even look back.

In Florida, it did not take long before I got myself another rock music DJ job, this time in West Palm Beach. I suppose this illustrates how volatile, foolish, and irresponsible I was. As I reflect on it now, I think I could not appreciate a good job when I had one. The job I walked away from with WAVZ was a coveted position for nearly anyone interested in rock music radio. But I was intolerant and maybe even a little arrogant. It was generally the way my life was in my early radio days: gypsy, volatile, and wild.

Groupies

My rock radio days were also marked by my introduction to groupies. Everyone who has ever worked in radio has stories about groupies. These are people who become enamored with your voice and your personality as they perceive it while listening to you on the air. In my case, as is the case with most male radio personalities, then and now, there were female groupies. They chased after me like flies after molasses. In many cases, they actually stalked me. They would call me, they would wait outside of the radio station, sometimes in the parking lot, waiting for me after I would get off the air. Then they would approach me, and I must admit, I let a number of them catch me.

I don't claim to understand how the minds of these people worked. But I got the impression they created some fantasies in their minds and wanted to fulfill them in some way by getting involved with me. I don't know. But I was young, single, and very much interested in women. It was difficult to resist young, attractive women who virtually threw themselves at me. I am not boasting, nor am I proud of what I did; I'm simply relating a colorful reality of my profession.

Rescuing the Amerasian Orphans

Probably the most memorable occasion in my rock radio years came when I was working for KENI in Anchorage, AK, I did a morning show. Actually, it was a long road for me. I began by doing a rock and roll show from seven to midnight which was a big smashing success. After about a year and a half of that, the program director of the station, Bob King, who I became great friends with, trained me and then turned the morning show over to me. So I was waking up Alaska every morning with a free form radio program: music, talk, etc. The end of the Vietnam War was at hand and all of the news every morning was about the horrible last days of Saigon.

As the Communists were closing in on Saigon, there were endless stories that made hot news, but were tragic and sad. One of the news items happened to be about Amerasian children. It suggested that, as the Communists were closing in, they would treat the Amerasian children very poorly and might even kill them. Because of my involvement in Vietnam and because of my memories, I began to talk about it on the air. I said, "You know, these children are the product of our involvement in Vietnam. They're innocent children and they are not going to be treated well by the Communists."

There was a story about a specific orphanage in Saigon holding about 120 children and they were almost all Amerasians. I guess my heart opened and I felt some responsibility, as all Americans probably should have. I said on the air, "We should try to do something; I don't know what, but something. I am tired of just talking about it and not doing anything." The audience was so caught up in it that the phones at the radio station began to ring off the hook. I never intended it, but people started sending in donations and it got out of hand very quickly. I certainly was not prepared to coordinate an effort of the kind we were contemplating. Our saviors became the Anchorage Jaycees, who volunteered to coordinate the collection of the money which, before we knew it, was in excess of $200,000. We were able to get an airplane, fly to Saigon, and pick these kids up, and, were in fact, one of the last planes out. We flew back to California and there was a brief stay there before we flew to the East Coast, where the children were, for a very short time, placed in an orphanage. Finally, they were adopted out to parents all across America.

An interesting follow-up to this story is that about three years ago, a young man who was one of the orphans wanted to find out his origins in this country. Working through the Anchorage Daily News, he found out who I was, how it all happened, and how he arrived in America. The Anchorage newspaper called KENI, which is currently one of my affiliates (is this not a small world?) and the young man was given my phone number. I guess I cannot remember a more emotional moment when he said, "I want to thank you for getting me out of Saigon, for the wonderful American parents I have, and for the wonderful American education." I felt like I actually did something. It wasn't just me; it was the people of Alaska who opened their hearts and wallets.

9-1-1 Dispatch

There were sometimes phases I went through of being burned out and disgusted with radio. One of them came about when I was about 30 and living in Castroville, California and so I got a job in Monterey County as a 911 dispatcher. I thought that this would be a stable job and of course, my voice was an asset in acquiring the position. I was required to keep track of the whereabouts of 15 or 20 police cars throughout the city. Though there were supervisors on duty, generally you would take a call from someone screaming on the phone that someone was dying, or choking to death or that a house was on fire or someone was breaking into their home. You were required to determine what the appropriate response was and dispatch it. There were nights I came home and had nightmares, I had cold sweats, I would wake up in the middle of the night screaming. I did the job for a year and finally left because I just couldn't do it anymore.

In one instance of working as a dispatcher, an officer in Seaside, California was shot in the stomach when I was on duty. He had been shot several times and he had somehow crawled to his car and was whispering for help into his microphone. I couldn't take it. I thought about it and I thought, 'I'm not making enough money — nobody is — to do this.' That is a very difficult job to learn because you have to mentally learn to hear many different things at one time. Your brain actually has to be trained to think this way. There were too many situations in which what I did directly affected whether someone lived or died. I have a lot of respect for people who do that. I go on the radio and I may live or die in front

142

of an audience, but I have a reasonable hope that what I do is not going to get someone killed.

A Change in Life Direction

By about 1975, I reached a point in my experience with radio when I got tired of it. I suppose I started to get bored with the rock music radio shtick, I was getting tired of the gypsy lifestyle, and I knew that I wasn't going to get rich doing this. Or maybe I was just getting too old for this gig and I wanted a change.

7

TALK RADIO

The period of my life before I seriously entered into the world of talk radio was one of transitions. I was constantly in search of something more than just an average job. Thus, I spent this time of my life picking up one job, growing bored, finding another, and so on. As I have said, I love electronic and technical things. I am intrigued by how they work and I love the challenge of fixing them. After twenty years of intellectually non-challenging rock radio, and its inherently gypsy-like existence, I needed something different, challenging, and perhaps more secure. So I took this technician job at Cox Cable in San Diego. I was there for about three years, and fell from a telephone pole, injuring my back. It was also about that time I began to develop an interest in satellite technology and thought about leaving Cox Cable. Fortunately, an acquaintance of mine was into satellite technology and advised that I try to get a job working with Times-Mirror Corporation at their new installation located in Las Vegas.

My work at Times-Mirror was actually exciting at first. We had to basically build the whole cable station system from scratch. This meant I installed all the satellite gear, the processing and microwave lengths, and all the other equipment for the cable system. Then, after building the cable system, I maintained it. I kept this job for about five years. I must say the first two years on this job were the most exciting because the technology was new and we were experimenting with everything to make this whole system work. I was what was called the headend technician, and this was actually a high level job. An entire department worked under me and I had an excellent salary.

Unfortunately, once the whole system was built, it turned into a kind of Maytag repairman syndrome. In my position, I could delegate all the work. Only occasionally did I get involved in work that was really fascinating. It was only a matter of time before my boredom nearly overwhelmed me and I began to again yearn for something that would not only satisfy my talents in electronics, but sustain my interests more permanently as well.

The Road to KDWN

My wife at the time, Kim, did not share my philosophy about work. As far as she was concerned, I should be content with a secure, well paying job in a big multi-national company. Maybe she was just more practical-minded then me. She just wanted me to make good money, have regular hours, and dedicate my life to her and our family when I was not working. Well, this just wasn't me. I cannot stay with anything very long that does not excite me in some way. I needed intellectual stimulation and I needed to do something for which I had a genuine interest or curiosity. Just sitting around and collecting a check was not for me. Kim just did not understand my thinking on this.

It was about this time that, as I was whiling away my life at Times-Mirror, word got out to Claire Reese, the program director of KDWN, the Las Vegas, Nevada radio station. KDWN is a huge, clear channel, 50,000 watt radio station. With its strong signal, KDWN has an impressive broadcast range which reaches up to about 150 miles around Las Vegas. This, of course, includes the highway from Los Angeles, which is significant because of the many people driving up to Las Vegas.

At night, KDWN is an altogether different radio station. Radio signals behave somewhat differently as they bounce off the ionosphere and can broadcast much further, particularly when you have a very strong signal to begin with, as is the case with KDWN. At night, the 50,000 watt signal of KDWN broadcasts to 12 western states. Obviously, with this type of broadcast range at night, it has a tremendous opportunity to reach many more people than just Las Vegas and the highway from Los Angeles.

Apparently, Claire Reese had heard that I had many years of radio experience, with a certain amount of experience in talk radio. In essence, KDWN found me. I didn't even know they were looking for anyone. Claire Reese was very clever in her approach, inviting me to do some part-time work for KDWN.

"Wouldn't you like to work in radio again, at least part of the time? We sure could use the help," she said persuasively. She appealed to my deepest instincts, and I could not resist.

"Sure," I said.

And that was that.

So, one day, they put me in with another talk show host on a Saturday show, just to see how I would work out. Normally, I don't like working with anyone else; I prefer working alone on the air. For one thing, with two radio hosts, one tends to dominate the other, or possibly the two will start to argue, or if there is a caller on the line who is put on the air, both may give the impression of ganging up on the caller, and so on. In this case, I got along very well with this particular host. His name was Jack Daniels, like the whiskey. To this day, Jack remains one of my dear friends. After this initial show as my audition, Claire Reese came to me in the studio.

"You did pretty well," Claire said. "Why don't you do a little more work for us?"

I was immediately offered a part time, weekend shift as part of a two-man talk show, which I gladly accepted. And I must say, I had a terrific time; it was a lot of fun. Alas, that same old black magic of radio put its spell on me; I was hooked all over again. All the while,

I continued to work at Times-Mirror during the week, working a regular five day week. Eventually, I was offered a midday talk show, to be aired every weekday, co-hosting with Jack Daniels from 10 am to 2 pm. I was eager to do this, although I still preferred working alone. But Jack and I more or less complimented each other, a critical necessity if a two-man talk show is to succeed.

Nonetheless, I needed to figure out what to do about my job at Times-Mirror. So, I talked to management there, and told them that KDWN wanted me to do this show, and I needed to work there from 10am to 2pm. Much to my amazement, Times-Mirror said go ahead. Only, to keep my end of the bargain, I had to work at Times-Mirror from 3pm to 11pm. This meant I would have to work 12 hours every day of the regular work week. This turned out to be grueling for me. Somehow, I managed to work like this for about six months.

The Turning Point at KDWN

Just as I was at my physical and mental limits after six months of this madness, Times-Mirror management came to me and gave me an ultimatum. They wanted me to make a choice. I had to choose to either go to KDWN, or manage the technical department I ran exclusively for Times-Mirror and climb the corporate ladder. I told them I would think about it. And I thought about it. I thought about it until I agonized over it. Then I went to talk to Claire Reese. Claire wanted me to work for KDWN exclusively. She made me an offer, but unfortunately, her offer was a good $8,000 less than what I was making at Times-Mirror. This was a big decision at this point in my life. Do I leave a perfectly good, secure, well-paying job for a radio job that paid significantly less and which was not necessarily very secure? After meeting with Claire, I went home to talk to my wife. Kim just thought I was absolutely, completely out of my mind. To her, there was no alternative to Times-Mirror. Nonetheless, in the end, I went with my first love: radio.

There I was again, back in radio full time. To start, I continued with the show I co-hosted with Jack Daniels, from 10am to 2pm. I also did the necessary production work including commercials and whatever else needed to be done for several months.

Now, KDWN was plagued by a great deal of paid programming. Paid programming is when someone pays for a certain amount of airtime to do a show. For example, a local chiropractor might pay for 30 minutes of airtime to do a show in which he pitches his practice. Or the local bowling alley would pay to do a show on bowling. For the station, this type of paid programming did not go long on ratings, but it did make money. The trouble was that often the airtime used conflicted with our regularly scheduled show. We might go on the air for an hour, but this would be interrupted with a 30-minute show on bowling, or gardening, or whatever. Then, we would resume the regular show, disrupting any flow that may have been generated during the first part of our show. This only hurt our show and no doubt our ratings, too. But we put up with this and tried our best to make a good show despite the interruptions.

Claire Reese & Nighttime Radio

After a few months, I started to dream about doing a night show. I was very much aware of how powerful a station KDWN was, and how widely it was broadcast at night. I wanted to reach more people; I was ambitious, as always and I wanted to take advantage of the nighttime opportunity. I told Claire Reese that I wanted a chance to do a show at night. She listened carefully, nodded and then said: "We'll see." And that was that.

Claire Reese is one of the most unusual people I have ever known in my whole life. This is a person I would grow to love and to hate at the same time. I love her because she is one of the most professional, intelligent, hard-bitten business people I have ever known. Claire Reese is every inch a radio person. She possesses an unbelievable amount of knowledge and experience about the business of radio. Yet, at times, Claire Reese is also as mad as a hatter. Over the course of the years I worked at KDWN, Claire Reese fired me many times. She would probably acknowledge many of the instances when she fired me, but she would probably *deny* many more. I think it safe to say my relationship with Claire Reese was a love/hate relationship. And I'm sure this is on both sides. I'm sure there were times when Claire Reese hated my guts, but she recognized my talent right from the beginning, and for that she loved me.

Well, there was a five-hour show, from 1am to 6am every day, hosted by an older man, I'll call him Hank Brandon. Hank had been in broadcasting for many years, spending many years doing this show. But Hank was considering retirement, so there was a chance that eventually, if I hung around long enough, I could have a shot at possibly taking over his show. Hank obviously could care less about this program; he had several lines to receive calls, but he would either neglect callers altogether, or he would do his show a long time before he even got to callers. Usually, on any given night, Hank would just sit down in front of the microphone, take out the local paper, and literally read each article as it appeared in the paper. Sometimes, you could actually hear the newspaper pages rustle. Nothing could be more boring and it was no surprise that the program was not very popular to listeners. Obviously, there had to be a change there, and I was willing to bet that Claire Reese probably recognized this.

Art Bell: Live at Night

One day, I got my break. It turned out that Hank got sick and could not come in to do the show. Claire came to me and told me now was my chance. She warned me that if I did a lousy job, the big hook would come and I would be yanked right out of there. I thanked Claire and was very excited at the opportunity to do my own live, all night talk show. This was fantastic. I knew I could do a good job. Then Claire explained to me how important the show was to the station. Believe it or not, although Hank's show was not a very good one, it was important to the station because of the expanded nighttime audience.

When the importance of what she had told me really settled in, I started to panic for some reason. In fact, this situation induced in me my first pre-talk show panic attack. I wanted desperately to do a good job; I wanted this to work more than anything. But now, just before the show, my heart started to pound furiously, breathing was difficult, I began to sweat profusely, I was shaking, and I smoked one cigarette after the other just to survive. Finally, at 1am, it was my turn to go on the air. By this time I was thoroughly soaked from perspiration and nervous as hell. Unfortunately, I don't have tapes of the first few shows, but I am certain I sounded very, very nervous and scared.

I began the show amidst my panic attack, but somehow I went forward. I think the only thing that had a way of soothing me, and encouraging me, was the listener response. Poor Hank Brandon would not only drone on, but often he never even solicited listeners to call. And when he did, no one might call for an hour at a time. I made every effort to be well prepared and when I went on the air, I just began discussing topics of interest at the time. I was ready for anything, and the moment I invited listeners to call, the phone bank lit up like a Christmas tree. The phones were jammed with callers throughout the night. I had a blast. Claire Reese was pleased.

Nighttime Success

Two weeks passed after my first shot at doing this all night talk show. Then I had another chance at it. Again, I was well prepared for the show, I talked about what was of interest at the time, and the phone bank lit up like a Christmas tree. That's what did the trick for me and that's when the change occurred. Claire Reese now knew that she had a hit on her hands with me. Poor Hank was shifted to do the day show, and I got to do the night show. This was the beginning of a show called *West Coast AM*.

The Plaza's Dripping Ceiling

There are a number of interesting stories about *West Coast AM* from when we first got started. For one thing, at that time, KDWN was located in the Las Vegas Plaza Hotel. And as part of a trade-off for advertising the hotel on the air, the Plaza Hotel provided the toll free 800 number used on the air during my show. For years, when Hank gave the 800 number on his show, it was hardly ever used. On average, the 800 number phone bill was maybe $100 per month. The Plaza Hotel didn't think anything of paying this bill. But after I was on the air for one month, they got the bill, only this time it was for $12,000! Plaza Hotel management went through the roof. Of course, they immediately pulled the 800 number. KDWN had to get its own 800 number to accommodate all the calls I was getting, and there were many of them.

One night when I was doing my show at the Plaza Hotel I suddenly felt something drip on my head. Drip, drip, drip. I touched my head and looked up to discover that it was some strange liquid seeping from a crack in the ceiling. This was so disconcerting to me as I proceeded with my show that I related it to my listeners.

"You're not going to believe this, but my ceiling seems to be dripping," I said on the air.

The dripping did not let up, so I got up and sort of stood to one side near the microphone and tried to continue doing my show. But the dripping seemed to get worse. Drip, drip, drip, and more drips, and more drips. Now the stuff from the ceiling was dripping on my equipment. The board and the electronics in the studio were getting these drips, and I began to panic.

"Oh my God," I exclaimed on the air. "I'm going to get electrocuted; these drips are getting on my equipment."

Drip, drip, drip. I was now up and wandering around, still talking to my listeners, while I was trying to look into our adjacent production studio, which I could see through a pane of glass that divided me from this studio. I thought, "Oh my God, now there is dripping coming through the ceiling in the production studio!" The awful drips were getting on the equipment in the other room. I also noticed that drips were getting on the stuff in the VIP room, the newsroom, the whole place was dripping. I freaked out. My listeners freaked out. I got on the phone with Claire Reese. I was panicked and she began to panic. She got in her car and drove down to the station.

In the meantime, everyone was calling maintenance at the hotel to find out what was going on. I then received a call from the owner of the station, Bob Blanch, who facetiously called me on a private line and told me that there was a 200,000 gallon swimming pool right above my head. This did not help things. Mr. Blanch just laughed, and laughed, and laughed. He rarely chided me, but this time he couldn't help himself for some reason. I continued to panic and tried my best to keep the show going without getting electrocuted. I went to commercial breaks over and over again. To avoid electrocution or the destruction of the equipment, Claire Reese had thrown blankets over everything. The dripping continued, and I ended up trying to hold my ground for about an hour and a half.

Finally, hotel maintenance sent two guys to investigate the damage. By this time, I had taken a moment to examine this peculiar, nasty looking liquid more closely. I noted that it was a brownish, murky color. In fact, it looked like there was brownish, murky particulate matter suspended in the liquid. I assumed that if this were pool water, it was probably just getting dirty as it passed through the ceiling. Beyond that, I didn't give it much more thought.

The maintenance men wandered around the studio, and I thought, "Why not put these guys on the air?" I had been receiving a barrage of calls from my listeners, and it was clear to me that they were totally involved and interested. I turned to the maintenance guys and asked them if they would object to going on the air to explain to my listeners what was going on. At first they were hesitant, then one of them agreed to go on. We went on the air and

I asked the man to explain in simple, non-technical layman's terms what was going on.

"Well, sir, up above us there," the man said thoughtfully, pointing towards the ceiling. "Uh, there's a commode that backed up."

I looked blankly at him in disbelief as I considered all the havoc that had occurred within the last couple of hours.

"You mean, a toilet overflowed?" I asked, paraphrasing what he had said to make sure I fully understood this revelation.

"Yes, sir."

There it was. Now the whole world knew that a horribly backed up toilet had showered its contents on my head. I was greatly embarrassed and disgusted by all this. By morning, when I got off the air, I got home as quickly as I could to rinse myself off from this foul mess. Not long afterwards, Claire Reese was screaming and yelling on my phone. Apparently, once the Plaza Hotel management learned I had broadcast that the hotel's plumbing went bad, they immediately wanted to kick our radio station out of the building. As far as they were concerned, we were, in essence, advertising that the hotel was a dump. Claire Reese was beside herself over this. I thought, oh boy, not only did I probably lose my job, but I probably lost everyone else's job because the lease was canceled.

Fortunately, after all the excitement had subsided, and everyone calmed down, the Plaza Hotel management was remiss and decided not to cancel the lease after all. I kept my job, and so did everyone else. This was one more of a number of odd behind-the-scenes radio adventures I'll never forget.

Thermos O' Glass

When I commuted the 130 miles round trip between Pahrump and KDWN in Las Vegas, I always carried with me a thermos bottle of coffee. It was back when thermos bottles were made with a glass container inside and a metallic or plastic sheath outside. I was sitting in the studio at about two or three in the morning drinking coffee, as usual. After consuming about half of the coffee, I looked down into my cup — I had dropped my thermos bottle earlier and hadn't bothered to check it — and what did I see floating around and on the bottom of the cup but what I thought was ground glass. I reached over and shook the thermos bottle and I could hear bits of glass bouncing around. Well, in my own mind, that meant I had been drinking ground glass for the last two hours. I panicked. On the air. "Ladies and gentlemen, I've been drinking ground glass for the last two hours." People started calling me saying, "Quick, get off the air and get to a hospital." They had emergency medical teams showing up at the Plaza Hotel; it was awful. But I refused to leave.

People were calling me and advising me on the air about what to do. One guy called up and said, "I can save your life. You need to eat half a loaf of bread, at least half a loaf of bread." I guess the assumption was that the bread would go into my stomach, absorb the broken glass, and it would pass that way harmlessly through my system. I was ready to do anything. Someone ran up to the radio station and left a loaf of bread outside the station door. I ran out and got it, ran back into the studio, and ran three minutes of commercials. In three minutes, I was able to down half a loaf of bread. It was the ugliest thing you ever saw; I was stuffing pieces of bread into my mouth a mile a minute.

I came back on the air, bloated with coffee and now the bread expanding in my belly, and I had the worst bellyache I ever had in my life. Even though I thought I was dying, I stayed on the air until the bitter end. People were telling me it was the end, they were calling up saying, "Goodbye;" it was really pathetic.

After I got off the air, I looked very carefully and found that yes, the thermos bottle had indeed broken. However, the glass had stayed inside the area between the glass and the outside of the container. What I was actually drinking were little paint chips that had coated the glass. Another radio story that was not so funny at the time, but now it is.

Good Job, You're Fired

I did the *West Coast AM* show for more than a decade. And over the years, the show always ranked number one on the West Coast as an all night talk show. I was and still am one of the only very successful radio talk show hosts to do unscreened, live talk radio. I do not screen the calls I receive. Which means I never know what to expect the next time I press the caller button and someone goes on the air. It has always been my philosophy to do it this way. I take a risk in doing this, but it makes it interesting, spontaneous, and I handle everything as it comes along. Usually, I don't even limit the topic of discussion. If someone calls and wants to talk about a particular topic, then that's what we do. And unlike some talk show hosts, I don't need to talk only to people who happen to agree with me on a topic. Everyone is welcome to call. I know myself; if I did not operate this way, I would get bored, and I would not have stayed with it as long as I have.

Now, despite all the success *West Coast AM* was having, Claire Reese still found reasons to fire me, many times. The last most memorable example was after I had just flown to Paris, France on the Concord and returned from that trip. The flight on the Concord was a fantastic experience, and seeing Paris was wonderful, too. I made it all part of my show. I returned with the intent to share with my listeners my experience. But by the time I got back, what with jetlag and so on, I simply was too exhausted to do the show right away. I needed some rest, so I called Claire Reese.

"Claire, I can't come in to do the show tonight, I'm dead tired," I said wearily.

"Well, fine," she cranked back. "Then don't come back in at all."

She hung up the phone in my ear. She was not joking; she was quite earnest when she said this. Three hours later, she called back. "All right," she said. "You're not fired. Skip tonight, come in tomorrow, and I'll either find someone for tonight, or I'll shut the station down entirely." Claire Reese was often melodramatic and frequently threatened to shut the radio station down. This, of course, was ridiculous, but she said these sorts of things.

"No, that's all right," I said, incensed. "I'll come in anyway. So, in I went.

Claire Reese was also a screamer. Sometimes, I would wake up in the middle of the day to her voice screaming on my answering machine about something I had done or she thought I had done. She had a personality that could piss off the pope and a taskmaster way about her. She would sit at her desk, and look over her glasses on the bridge of her nose, and give you a look meaner than any one of the meanest teachers or principals you could encounter at school. Usually, this look was delivered along with a tirade of words that would make a sailor blush. There had been occasions when I would sit in her office and she would use every name in the book to address me. Oddly enough, she respected my talent and I respected her leadership. She may not be a good manager, but she is definitely a good leader. I also think she has a soft heart.

Sometimes when I think of Claire Reese, I think of the "Lou Grant" television series in which Mrs. Pinchaw, the owner of the TV station, would sit in her home with her poodle, dictating to the world. Although this may not exactly be Claire Reese, it is not too far from the truth. Claire sits at her desk as one would sit on a throne. And by God, you better listen to what she has to say. I must say, over the years I was utterly terrified of this woman. She would scream and yell and I would quiver and be appropriately scared and frightened. Eventually, after enough years had gone by, I began to realize I did not have to take this type of treatment and I started yelling back. This, in turn, resulted in a number of pitched screaming and yelling battles. I matched her decibel for decibel and word for word. This, in turn, resulted in my being fired even more times. Claire Reese does not like being corrected or challenged in any way. She's a queen, a ruler, and you just don't do that sort of thing. But I did it.

Raised Off the Air

One day, long after *West Coast AM* had proven itself a popular show, I went into Claire Reese's office and explained to her that I desperately needed a raise. Up until then, I was going along, scraping out a living as best I could on the salary they gave me, but it was not enough. I was aware that despite the popularity of the show, the show did not make a lot of money. For some reason, the sales department of KDWN did not try to sell the show. As far as I was concerned, *West Coast AM* was definitely a marketable commodity, and prime for syndication. Anyway, I went into Claire's office and tried to get the raise I not only thought I deserved, but desperately needed.

"No," was Claire Reese's reply to my request. "Can't do it."

I was dumbfounded. I couldn't believe it.

"Well, if you can't do it," I said steadily, trying to maintain my composure, "I can't continue here."

"Fine, then don't," Claire Reese said firmly.

In this instance, I quit and she fired me, both at the same time. In a sense, we were at another stand off. This is a very famous time in my experience with KDWN that many of my longest listeners will recall. They will remember when I did not come on the air. And some may even remember how long I quit KDWN, which I believe was about four months. The crazy thing about it is that I ended up working for another radio station in Las Vegas, for not much more money, and I didn't even do a show. In fact, I stayed off the air during that four-month hiatus and I became the chief engineer of that radio station.

Forced to Grovel

In the meantime, Claire Reese kept *West Coast AM* on the air, but she used a couple of other talk show hosts in an attempt to do it. Unfortunately for her, my replacements could not do as good a job as I did. I'll even say they failed miserably. And for the entire period while I was away, KDWN constantly received calls from listeners asking about my whereabouts. Where did Art Bell go?

They wanted to know. I'm happy to say the show was awful. And I am certain Claire Reese knew it. No doubt her pride prevented her from asking me to come back.

I tried to hold out as long as I could. But eventually I gave in. This engineering stuff wore on me. I tried calling Claire Reese to ask for my job back. She ignored my calls. After a few days, I called her and she answered them. But when I asked for my job back, she declined to let me have my job. Her pride was too great to rehire me. I would not be put off. So, I kept calling her. Every time she got back on the phone, I told her, "I want to get back, I want to get back on. I know I made a mistake and I want to get back on."

"No," she would say.

I continued to call Claire Reese every day. Would she ever admit she made a mistake? No-o-o-o. I swallowed my pride and I told her I made the mistake. It's true; I gave Claire Reese an ultimatum and I knew she never responded favorably to ultimatums. I explained to her I should never have left. I groveled. Finally, she called me and said, "All right, damn it, you can come back."

And back I came to continue doing *West Coast AM*. This time I did the show six nights a week, a total of 30 air hours every week. I kept this up for the next two or three years, very successfully, achieving the highest ratings. The phone lines were packed every night and the show was as popular as it could be. Now, I lived in Pahrump at that time, which meant I had to drive 65 miles to Las Vegas one way, and 65 miles back home, six days a week. All this airtime and all this driving was too much for me. I realized I could not do it indefinitely and survive. Again, I found myself standing before Claire Reese's desk.

"Claire, I can't operate like this anymore. I need to cut my air time back to a five day week," I said wearily. "I need a little bit of my life back." Somehow I managed to avoid getting fired over this and was actually able to cut back to a five-day week. It was still a lot of commuting.

No News, I'm Outta Here

Nonetheless, eventually I did manage to get fired again despite my success. This time it was not by Claire Reese, but by the elderly, eccentric, lovable millionaire, who owned the station, Bob Blanch. I believe he's in his eighties at the time of this writing. In those days, Bob Blanch owned a number of radio and television stations. Anyway, he just happened to drop by KDWN one day, and called me into his office.

"Art," he said, "I've decided that we need to cancel the news."

I looked at him in confusion. For five minutes, at the top of every hour, we had the Associated Press news. No one cancels the news. It's part of the way you do radio. Besides, I did a show which required being aware of what was going on in the world, and the news break was the only time I could run to the men's room to take care of business, and run back to the studio to continue the show.

"Ah, but sir, you can't drop the news," I said, respectfully.

"Yes, I can," he contested almost jocularly.

"But wait a minute," I said, fretting, "I have to go to the men's room. And the only time I can do that is during the news, at the top of the hour. You can't cancel the news."

"Yes, I can drop the news," he insisted. "I own the station, and if I want to drop the news, I'll have it dropped."

"Well, if you cancel the news, you'll have to fire me."

"Okay," he said. "Then you're fired."

"Okay," I said. I started to walk out of the door.

"Wait a minute," he said as I was leaving. "Okay, you're not fired."

In the end, Bob Blanch listened to reason and we did not cancel the news. But it was an awfully strange encounter with this man who I hardly ever saw, and yet he was behind my success and was literally the one who fed me.

Learning from the Screamer

Overall, my experience at KDWN was a rocky, lovable time that I will never forget. Moreover, it is really where I got started in talk radio, and for that I will always be indebted to the people at KDWN, especially to Claire Reese. Sometimes, as I reflect on my experience at KDWN, I compare it to my experience at boot camp when I enlisted in the Air Force. Claire Reese was the "get in my face" drill sergeant, who drilled and pounded into me what I needed to know for my career. Of course, KDWN became more than just basic training because I learned more than just the basics to succeed in my business.

One good example of what I learned from Claire Reese was that I should always err on the side of caution. That I should avoid putting something on the air that could get me sued or which could get the radio station sued. This was good advice, especially these days in this litigious society in which we live. For this advice and direction, and a whole lot of other good advice and direction, I owe a lot to Claire Reese. She may feel that what I have said here is not true or it is too critical, but I have only related the facts as they are from my perspective. At any rate, I respect Claire Reese immensely, no matter what she has done in the past or does in the future.

My Philosophy of Talk Radio

First and foremost, I believe that talk radio should be an open medium. A talk radio program should offer a forum to discuss a variety of topics and not just politics. Most radio programs, even very popular radio programs, put emphasis almost entirely on politics. Rush Limbaugh is one example of this. In a way, I feel sorry for Rush Limbaugh, because he has to face three inevitable hours of politics every single day. Politics is a good and important topic to discuss. And God knows I am a political animal. I enjoy discussing politics on the air. But limiting a radio program to only politics gets boring.

160

Ramona in front of Thai temple.

Communist Chinese guard; note automatic shotgun.

McDonald's in Tokyo, Japan.

This is the Russian Armory which houses the Crown Jewels of Russia.

Me, my son Art IV and Bob Crane

Entering the Yukon Territory in Canada.

Ramona and I in beautiful Alaska. Look at the glaciers in the background.

The Sphinx and I.

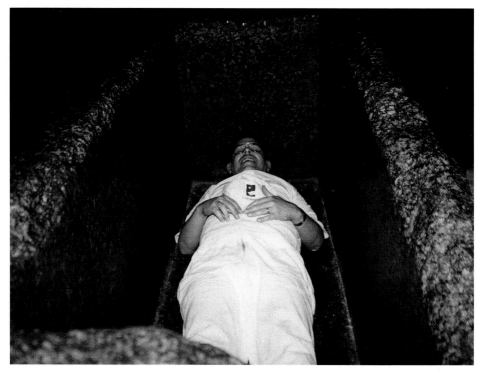

That's me in the King's sarcophagus, deep within the King's pyramid.

In Giza on a camel

Entryway to a sealed area of the Giza pyramid not open to the public.
We entered with Zahi Hawass, Director of Antiquities.

Ramona and an Israeli soldier in Jerusalem, foraging for food,

In Pompeii, surveying the ruins.

Spotted this girl on the island of Rhodes off the coast of Greece.

More beautiful women from Indonesia, Thailand and China.

445 foot formation found August 8, 1993, in wheat field in Cherhill, England.

The figures you see in this photo were not there when the photo was taken; note the apparent "revolutionary" costume and possible dark figure near the bridge.

My philosophy is that a radio program should be open. I like surprises. I don't always want to know what to expect; that's the way I like it. I don't want to know what's going to happen until it happens on the air. This does not mean I don't prepare for my program. In fact, I spend about five hours every day preparing. I am continually in touch with the world, with CNN, with a variety of news services, and with on-line information services available 24 hours a day. I also solicit and receive dozens and dozens of faxes from everywhere and from many different people about what's going on in the world. I am prepared, but I do not allow my preparedness to interfere with what people want to talk about when I get on the air. This is why I am adamant about not screening my calls.

The Flexible Host

I do not have a call screener. Rush Limbaugh and many other talk show hosts screen their calls. Rush even boasts of the fact that he screens calls, and often carries on conversations on the air with his call screeners. He also admits that he only wants callers on the air who make him look good. I don't do any of this; it's just not my style. I have many call lines, but I have five main lines. And I just reach down and punch the next button that lights up. To some degree, this is a very dangerous form of talk radio, but it's completely spontaneous and honest. If the caller is mean-spirited or boring, I may blow them off quickly. For obscene callers, I do protect my listeners to an extent with a seven-second delay that enables me to disconnect them instantly.

I think in talk radio, a good talk show host can take a bad call and make it informative, entertaining, or in some way useful and worth listening to. That takes interaction between the host and the caller. As far as I'm concerned, que sera, whatever will be, will be. This makes it fun for me and for my listeners. And this is the thing that has sustained me through so many years in talk radio.

As I have indicated, only talking politics becomes boring, especially since there is so much else in life to talk about. You can

161

discuss love and human relations, all sorts of news items that fascinate people, and many interesting current events. This is why I discuss things like asteroids which appear to threaten the earth, or why women spend so much time in the women's restrooms, or earthquake predictions, or unusual weather patterns, or UFO sightings, and on and on. I have also learned over the years how to keep a radio program flowing by maintaining a good pace of going from one caller to the next.

Short & Sweet, Fast & Fun

In the past, many talk show hosts had the tendency to spend too much time with any given caller. This slowed the pace of the exchange of ideas and conversation between the host and the caller, which makes a show boring. To curb this, someone, somewhere invented a special timer to remind the host that the time was drifting away. The timer consisted of a mechanism that emitted a tone that would begin as a low hum and lead to a shrieking noise towards the end of a three-minute period. The idea was that each caller would be limited to three minutes. Any time longer than three minutes, listeners would begin to lose interest anyway. The fact is the attention span of most listeners is very limited.

Well, I tried these timers for a while. Eventually, I realized I had an instinctive sense about when I should conclude a call. I did not need a timer. I automatically keep calls short, usually not more than three minutes, and sometimes as little as 10 or 15 seconds. This technique works. I determine the length of a call by how entertaining or informative a caller may be. And by experience, I know when a caller is entertaining or informative. Some people have complained that this makes me seem dictatorial and mean-spirited; this is not true. I must keep the show moving, and this really is the best way to do it. It is never my intention to deliberately insult anyone or treat anyone badly.

In short, talk radio should be fun, funny, sad, spontaneous, provocative, thoughtful, informative, entertaining, and above all *varied*. There should be *variety*. I believe the key to my success is the variety that is on my show. I admire Rush Limbaugh, but he limits himself with politics, although I think Rush is very funny and overall a great entertainer. I admire Howard Stern because he offers *variety* on his show. I even think Howard is a very, very funny man. He does tend to use bad language and tends to exhibit poor taste, but he really does not need to resort to this type of conduct because he is so naturally funny and entertaining without it. I believe if Howard dropped the bad language and poor taste, he would be even more widely accepted. This may sound stodgy, but that's how I view him and his show.

On one hand, I try not to take talk radio too seriously. I think it is important to approach talk radio with an upbeat, positive and fun attitude. On the other hand, I take talk radio very seriously. It's a very important part of my life and I love it. I feel extremely fortunate to have succeeded as I have, especially since I know there are many people in broadcasting who are very talented, maybe people who have a lot more talent than I have. And most of these people are starving to death out there in this business. Yet, these people are probably doing a wonderful job for very small audiences in their area. I pay tribute to these people here. I respect and admire the many dedicated people in radio, the thousands and thousands of them that are out there. I feel immensely blessed for having talent and good luck, particularly for the good luck in finding the many people who have been able to assist in my career.

It's Not as Easy as it Looks

I believe talk radio managers, and people who own radio stations which air talk radio programs, are very brave human beings. Radio is a very dangerous medium because if one person airs something libelous, the whole station could be sued into non-existence. Just having a license revoked would be enough to eliminate a radio station. I know that if I owned a radio station that aired talk radio I would have great trepidation. In fact, Claire Reese once intimated to me, after I had worked for her for eight years that it took that long before she could trust me on the air. She told me she finally could get some sleep at night. Apparently, until she trusted me, she had an uncanny way of sleeping with one ear listening to the radio at night and the other ear asleep.

There were many times when I would have a controversial sounding caller on the air, and I would immediately get a call on the hotline from her in the middle of the show to tell me to get that person off the air. Sometimes I listened to her sometimes I did not. I still admire her and Bob Blanch for their courage to air talk radio. And I admire other radio managers and owners for their courage to air talk radio.

Larry King

I believe I have assumed the position of filling the shoes of Larry King in all night radio. His are big shoes to fill. Larry King became very successful and popular with his radio program, virtually becoming a household name. And although he has gone on to CNN to do the very successful Larry King Show, he is known to look behind him at times. During a radio interview on Seattle's KVI, Larry King said something along the lines of "I regret leaving night time talk radio." Of course, I believe he did so for the money, which makes sense in a lot of ways.

King of the Night

My radio program, Coast to Coast AM, is the most predominant all night radio talk show in the country today with well over 400 affiliates at this writing. This puts me up in the top three positions for popularity among the most listened to talk radio programs in the country today. New affiliates are being added every couple of days or so. Larry King created a vacuum for me to fill when he vacated his nighttime spot. In a sense, his regret has become my good fortune; I filled what he has left. And for me, at this time in my career and at my age, this makes it a little easier to relax. Moreover, I am getting to the point where I say exactly what I feel on the air. Of course, I have always been honest with the people I talk to on the air. At a younger age, however, I would have been more cautious and less relaxed. At 53, I have become seasoned and better able to handle callers, and thus more inclined to speak my mind. Quite frankly, this makes my show better.

Why is Talk Radio Popular?

A recent national survey revealed that talk radio is America's number one format. When I started in talk radio, more than 12 years ago after twenty years of rock music radio, talk radio was an all but forgotten corner of broadcasting which consisted mostly of crack pots, maniacs, and the same dull voices droning on with nothing worth listening to. It has only been in the last several years that talk radio really caught fire. Larry King, of course, was around and had great popularity, but Rush Limbaugh also broke some ground by quickly gaining unprecedented popularity. While all this was going on, and talk radio was getting warmer and warmer, until it started on fire, particularly with Rush Limbaugh's success, I was forging ahead at KDWN with *West Coast AM*. Then, because I was at the right place at the right time, and Larry King gave up his reign in nighttime radio, my opportunity came.

But what was the reason for the fire? Personalities and the styles of certain personalities have a lot to do with the recent success of talk radio. For example, as I said earlier, Rush Limbaugh is a great entertainer; he's knowledgeable and has a great sense of humor. For those who want something a little more on the edge, Howard Stern is good entertainment, too. I have my own style and that appeals to many, many people. The other thing that is important is the subject matter. Rush has been very adept at politics, especially Republican politics. I offer variety. Air times also add to the popularity of talk radio. Rush is in the morning, G. Gordon Liddy is morning to afternoon, and I am late night to morning. We cover all the time periods throughout the day. There are markets for each of us and plenty of people who will listen.

I think, for the future, talk radio will continue to grow in popularity and it will become more diverse. Of course, talk radio has a lot of growing up to do, but it has great potential for success. One problem I see right now is that there are many people trying to copy Rush Limbaugh. I call them Rush Limbaugh clones. Yet, with all this copying, I don't think this is the direction of talk radio. I believe those who seek to follow such a direction are making a big mistake. A few of these clones will do moderately well, but the ones who will really succeed are those with originality and not the copycats. To excel, you must be individual, you must be unique, and you must not copy. Before I became a talk show host, I was a talk show listener and I still am. I listen to everyone, but I try not to listen too much to anyone in particular because I don't want to copy anyone.

Tom Leykis, Rush Limbaugh, G. Gordon Liddy...

Everyone has some opinion about their competitors, and I have my opinion about mine. Generally, I think it is unprofessional to be critical about my competitors. And I normally don't even say very much about them on the air, although the few times I have, it has been to compliment a competitor. I don't view my competitors with hostility, and in some cases I actually admire them.

Tom Leykis, for one reason or another, perceives me to be his enemy. I really don't understand how this got started, but for some reason, it's as though he just can't find enough reasons to dislike me. But then, I have come to realize that Leykis tends to enjoy taking shots at other talk show hosts, though I am one of his prime targets. Now, Tom Leykis is a liberal, and I am quite a middle-of-the-road conservative. So that's one legitimate difference we share and I certainly have no problem with that. I must admit, however, there have been times when he came close to pushing me over the edge with his slams against me and against my show. I eventually got to the point where I began to refer to him as the "great, incredible shrinking talk show," especially after receiving calls from my listeners who reported something nasty he had said about me on his show. Indeed, the fact is that I have actually replaced Leykis' show in a number of large US cities. Quite candidly, Leykis has been a sort of boil on my butt and nothing more significant than that. And one day it bursts and there is relief. As for his show, he screams his opinions; apparently he delivers at high decibel levels rather than high intellect levels. And that's enough of him.

G. Gordon Liddy, for my taste in talk show hosts, is a little stiff. He has definitely found his own niche in the radio world, and I wish him well. Nonetheless, he has uttered some things on the air that I would not have uttered. He has said things that were not really useful to anyone, and were probably said for the controversial or shock value. There is so much shocking stuff going on in the world today that there really is no need to generate our own shock as talk show hosts just to generate interest or ratings. It makes more sense to generate interest and ratings based on how we handle all the shocking stuff out in the real world. In other words, we should discuss the news and not make it by what we say.

Mike Reagan, the former president's son, appears to have carved out his own little niche in the radio world. But he is another one I find a little stiff. He'll go on the air and read senate bills or congressional bills introduced to his listeners. For me, that's a little boring. I would probably paraphrase a bill and then discuss the characteristics of a bill. But just reading something like that is somewhat dry.

Jim Bohanan is more on the liberal side of politics and thinking, but not very harmful. He is efficient and for a long time walked behind Larry King's shoes, but never quite filled them. Still, he has found his own little niche. The worst part of Bohanan is that he is not very entertaining. Furthermore, Bohanan poses a small threat to my show, because in many markets he is direct competition for me with his night airtime.

These radio talk show hosts I just mentioned are individuals with their own identities and are not caught up in the copycat mania. They have asserted their own personalities, have established their own formats, and have established their own niches. Of the many others that are out there, too many are just trying to copy someone else. This in the long run will most likely prevent them from achieving success. They will never be anything special, and they will never reach the top.

8

COAST TO COAST AM

Coast to Coast AM had its origin at KDWN as *West Coast AM*. I had been doing the show regularly, Monday through Friday, from 11pm to 4am (PST), for the better part of eight years. Then in 1988, I met Alan Corbeth, who was visiting Las Vegas while on business and made a point of meeting with me. I learned that he was an expert at syndicating radio programs and had been an avid listener of mine for the better part of a year after he had moved to Medford, Oregon. I met him and was delighted to discover what a nice guy he was. We both had a lot in common, radio being one thing in particular and we are also both very driven; I wanted to have a bigger show and Alan wanted to see me achieve this aim.

While he was visiting, I invited Alan to sit in on one of my shows. Afterwards, when Alan returned to Medford, we maintained contact. In the meantime, I sought to have Alan help out in an effort to syndicate my show and fortunately, I managed to persuade the investors who controlled my show to agree to get Alan involved. So Alan and I got to work to clear stations to run the show. After several months of feverish effort, we made it up to 17 stations when the investors involved made some deals that put control of the show in the hands of other investors. I was not comfortable with this arrangement and asked Alan to help if he could. We had a list of improvements we wanted to make, but no power to effect the change.

The challenge now was to push the show to the next level, which meant we needed to gain financial control. To do this, we spent the next several months securing investors of our own so we could buy controlling interest in the show. The moment we had done this, we were unbelievably excited because it meant we had the freedom to really get my show going. Both Alan and I set our sights on an overnight empire. No other network had tried to do what we were about to do, especially on such a big scale.

Don't Do It, Corbeth!

One week before Chancellor Broadcasting was to syndicate my show, Alan received a call from another network. Alan thought that perhaps another network executive was going to congratulate him on entering the sacred brotherhood of network radio. Instead, the man on the other end of the phone tried his best to discourage Alan and I.

"Corbeth, don't do it! Overnight radio is very difficult. Very, very tricky. As a matter of fact, none of us since Larry King have ever been able to do anything with overnight on a national level," this bigshot radio guy claimed. "More importantly, Corbeth, it's impossible to make any money. If you want to go broke, then don't listen to me."

We were not discouraged by the attempt to scare us into submission. At the time, Alan was confident that not only could a nationally syndicated overnight talk radio program succeed, but it could also result in a handsome profit, especially with Art Bell behind the microphone. He boasted that, apart from my performance, Chancellor Broadcasting had a very serious commitment to succeed by providing reliable program quality, consistent service, and would actually be interested in serving both our affiliates and our listeners.

We were definitely different than the major networks and I believe this was to our advantage. For one thing, most of the major networks, like NBC, ABC, CBS, Westwood One, and Mutual, already have long-standing affiliates, usually the big talkers in large markets. The difference with Chancellor is they were and continue to be open to both large and small markets. A second even more important factor is that many large networks at that time were and still are very close to crumbling under the weight and expense of their own top-heavy bureaucracy; they tend to be indifferent, inflexible, and arrogant. Third, the ineptitude, unreliability, dishonesty, and lack of professionalism of many of the smaller networks put the majority of talk stations around the country in a bind. Many of the small syndicators didn't then and still do not have engineering help available, they don't follow up on their affiliates' questions, and their programming is in some cases irresponsible and unreliable.

Beat the Clock

At the time of our acquisition, I was doing my show from KDWN in Las Vegas and the show was being fed to another Las Vegas studio. It was then sent across town via an eight-khz equalized telephone line. This is a rather old-fashioned analog telephone service that was once the backbone of the system by which networks fed their affiliates all over the country. From there, the signal went to BRN technical center in Colorado, where it was up-linked to a satellite. That situation was okay. It was the clock I could not wait to get rid of. The former owners had created this complicated, nonsensical way the commercial breaks were based on the hourly clock.

For the uninitiated, a network clock indicates where commercial breaks should occur. There are allotted time periods designated for the local stations for their own commercials, station identifications, and promotional announcements. Obviously, these breaks must fall within carefully designated time periods, or the local stations would

171

never know when to leave the network, and even worse, when to return without joining in the middle of something. What was frustrating about the network clock was that I could hardly say two sentences and it was already time for a commercial break. The clock in effect was ruining the flow of the show. I wanted the solitude of the night to contrast the changes and interruptions that are the norm during the daylight hours. Finally we changed the clock. Now we truly owned the night; I danced with joy.

Next on our list was the name of the show. As I mentioned a moment ago, it was called *West Coast AM* while I was at KDWN. But we aspired to greater things, a show that would cover the entire country. So, accordingly, we brazenly decided to call the show *"Coast to Coast AM with Art Bell,"* in anticipation of the day when we really would broadcast from one coast to the other. In fact, Alan Corbeth made a concerted effort to make sure I was heard on the East Coast.

One of the challenges in trying to get the East Coast was the fact that I had been airing at 4am east coast time; this is not a good time to start a show. So, to accommodate East Coast listeners, we decided that I should air the show at 11pm, which would give us the majority of the overnight period. The trouble with starting the show at this time at night was that we could not find a station in Las Vegas that could accommodate us; KDWN could not do it because they had commitments at 11pm. In the last year we have moved the time again, up to 10pm west coast time, in a further attempt to capture more of the opposite coast market.

The Homeless Radio Show

All of a sudden we found ourselves with a great show and nowhere to broadcast from. What should we do? Well, the options were not appealing. We could find another hotel to set up shop, or I could relocate to Medford, Oregon to use the network headquarters station. Chancellor Broadcasting, through its affiliation with the Talk Radio Network, had a full technical facility, administrative offices, and an earth station satellite up-link in Oregon. Logically, you might say I should have gone to Medford. Well, this is where Alan had the vision and the sense to realize it was to everyone's advantage to keep things the same as much as possible, not to change the show or its venue. That's when the decision to build a studio in my home was devised.

Building a studio was not an easy task. First there was the need to get a signal from Pahrump to Medford. We tried a couple of different types of technology. We wanted to use digital technology, but learned that the telephone company could not offer digital technology service until the year 2003. So, we decided on twisted pair cable technology. Then we found out that the telephone company wanted to charge us an outrageous $18,000 to install a couple of twisted wires two city blocks long. Finally, we decided to use a digital satellite up-link, and avoid the telephone companies altogether. Once all the other gear I needed was installed, I was ready to broadcast from home. My listeners never knew how much trouble it was to get on the air from my home. But once we got things going, we were pretty glitch free from then on.

Working from Home

I love doing *Coast to Coast* from home. Before I worked at home, I commuted 130 miles every day for years between my home in Pahrump and Las Vegas where KDWN is located. This was unnerving, exhausting, a strain, time consuming, and generally a royal pain; it made me miserable.

There is nothing better than working at home. At home I live in my own little world, in my own little atmosphere. Admittedly, this arrangement is a bubble of protection from the rest of the world. And yet I let the rest of the world in through various on-line computer services including the Internet, the World Wide Web, through CNN, through satellites of various types, through text news services, through Reuters Associated Press, through my computer electronic mail, through all these wonderful information superhighway sources. I am in touch with the world in just about every way you can imagine, even though I am in this little bubble of protection. But this lets me be myself. The outside influences are minimal, and then I go on the air and let it all hang out. It is marvelous.

I can walk from my living room and stroll to my studio that CBC built for me. The studio is modest, but I have everything I need to do my talk show. My satellite dish produces as good a quality as I would have if I were broadcasting from Westwood 1 in Studio City, or from any other major radio station in the country. Sometimes I think about my peers in this business like Rush Limbaugh. He says from time to time that it really does not matter where he is to do his show, as long as he is somewhere to do it. This makes me wonder why he would want to do his show from New York. It seems to me that New York would be an awful place to live and work, especially if you can live and work from anywhere to do what he does.

Working at home is great. I have all my comforts. I can pet my cats. My wife is at home with me either listening or safely asleep; this is comforting to me. She does either activity half the time. I can get up in the middle of my program and go out to the kitchen and grab some pretzels. I remember one time the news had about two minutes left, and for some reason I ran out to the kitchen for some pretzels. Well, I got to the kitchen to find a big bag of pretzels that only contained pretzel dust at the bottom. And I thought, 'What the hell.' So I up-ended the bag and put this pretzel dust in my mouth. It turns out that the pretzel dust was actually a mixture of 10% pretzel dust, and 90% salt. I thought I was going to die. I don't know how I managed to get back on the air two minutes later. I was choking, and coughing, and gagging. I now stay clear of pretzel dust. I also stay clear of dairy products, like milk. Milk has a way of creating mucus, which interferes with articulating clearly.

I get a sense of relaxation working at home with all those things and loved ones around which give me comfort. This helps me do a better program because it reduces my mental strain. Ultimately, I owe all this comfort and convenience to work from home to Alan Corbeth. He took the time to understand my personality, and had the vision to realize that the time and the investment it would take for me to operate as I do would pay off in the long run. It has paid off and it demonstrates that he knew what he was doing. I am immensely grateful for that.

Jacor

The breaking news at the time of this writing is that Chancellor Broadcasting/Talk Radio Network has been purchased by Premier Radio Networks. Premier is a wholly owned subsidiary of Jacor Communications, Inc., a company based in Covington, Kentucky, and is the number one syndicator of talk programming. Everyone tried to buy us all at once. We had overtures from Westwood One, ABC, CBS and Jacor. Jacor was the first, in terms of order, so we entered into a period of non-disclosure and as the others came along, we were not able to negotiate with them because we had entered into this non-disclosure agreement.

The deal was ongoing for many months. You can imagine the very weight of it, as hundreds of thousands of dollars in lawyers' fees and countless amounts of time and energy finally achieved the deal. The final deal was for approximately $9 million in cash so I guess it was worth waiting for, although the money is not going to change anything that I do or the way that I live.

Now you may say, Art, how could you have transferred over to a large corporation like Jacor? The answer is simple. Jacor is a very, very aggressive company, so they fit my personality perfectly. For that reason, I am glad that we ended up with Jacor. I think that there are a lot of other companies in the radio industry that don't particularly understand the business they are in. Jacor is particularly competent and I feel I can be represented well by them.

Jacor is also very happy to have Art Bell. They feel that they now have the Triple Crown of Radio: Laura Schlessinger, Rush Limbaugh and Art Bell. Because of the nature of AM nighttime radio, there's no place you can go and not hear me. That is why Jacor bought me—I am big, I'm a household name among my listeners and I have achieved tremendous success in my time slot. They see my success and they want to encourage and back it with the power of their corporation.

What About Chancellor Broadcasting?

Chancellor Broadcasting will continue to have a separate affiliate relations department, as the philosophy of Jacor is to leave something alone if it is working. Obviously, there are some functions, like accounting, etc. that will be handled by Jacor. But that is Jacor's reputation: they will not mess with something that works fine by itself. If a situation needs fixing, they will fix it. And that might mean a change in personnel, for instance. But Art Bell is proceeding nicely, I think. As far as Alan Corbeth is concerned, he will continue with Jacor as Vice President of Premier Radio Networks.

The Show's Popularity

To date, *Coast to Coast AM* is about six years old and broadcast in practically every major radio market in the country. Why is my show so popular? I have been asked many times recently why I think I have had such great success with *Coast to Coast*. The short answer to this is: I don't really know. But I do have some ideas why.

Winds of Change

Talk radio is the most listened to radio format in America today, but it won't stay that way unless it broadens its horizons and explores new ways of doing things. I think my show is leading talk radio along a more productive path for the long-term good of the radio industry as a whole. I believe that for talk radio to continue to be successful, whether it is my show or another, people need a more general reflection of life, something more spontaneous. That is why I would say that the most recent and now the best reason for the sharp increase in *Coast to Coast's* popularity is the direction in which I have taken the show in the last few years.

A few years ago, I began to see that people no longer felt what was going on in Washington was relevant to their daily lives. I knew that a year before the rest of the country knew it, so I started moving the show away from the humdrum of politics, which was just boring people. I am still a very political person, but I have unquestionably moved the show more in the direction of the paranormal. This is what people are interested in and this is where the controversy lies in the minds of my listeners.

I believe it is best not to limit yourself to the commonly accepted or politically correct definition of things unexplained or unproven. While I don't mind being on the edge as far as the media and the rest of society is concerned, I do have trouble with people who are not open-minded to things. I am not asking that everyone agree with what I say or the things my guests talk about on my show; I only hope that people are listening to both sides of an issue and not just making a snap decision about the way they feel about something.

When it comes to paranormal issues, such as the afterlife, extra-terrestrial intelligence, UFOs and the like, it is not whether *I* believe that it is true that is important or relevant; what matters is that there is a forum for these and other types of issues. This is one of the central reasons for my show's increased popularity.

Limitless Topics

I also think the show is popular because the show is unplanned, unregulated, the show may or may not be topical at any given broadcast, the show is fun, and my listeners have the freedom to direct the show. Many of my greatest competitors are limited by their own format while my show is not. For example, when *Coast to Coast AM* is picked up by a very large affiliate, which is in direct competition with another large affiliate in the city, perhaps one of the more influential stations in the area, I am not concerned. I know the people at most other stations limit themselves by dictating what callers can discuss on the air for a particular broadcast.

Rather than allow the listeners and callers to decide what they want to discuss, the average station will be very specific what the topic is for discussion, and anyone calling who does not adhere to this mandate, is immediately disqualified from getting on the air. Their host will say, "This hour, we're going to talk about gun control (or whatever else they decide)." And by God, if gun control is the topic, then no other topic shall be discussed. In other words, every call is carefully screened to make sure those calling don't try to talk about a different topic than the one stipulated. And even if a caller sounds boring, dumb or old, or is just in disagreement with the host, the call screener will not allow the caller on the air. This is very restricting; I don't believe this is how you should conduct a talk show.

Spontaneous & Unscreened

With my show, there is no caller screening, and even though I may bring up a topic of interest, if a caller wants to talk about something different, fine. This may seem an erratic and unprofessional way to conduct a radio program, but it has proven to be very effective in gaining listener support and interest. People want freedom; they don't want to be restricted. My program is completely open and spontaneous and I would not have it any other way. Having to deal with every manner of caller, from the intelligent, to the well read, to the imbibed, to the drug taker, to the callers talking about the strange, bizarre and unusual, to the callers with far out left or right opinions, I enjoy it. And from what I can tell, with comments and various correspondences from listeners, I know many, many listeners enjoy this format, too.

On TV some years back, there was a lady, I think her name was Betty Furness, who did a live commercial for a refrigerator. And she would extol the virtues of this refrigerator such as how big and spacious and well designed the thing was. Then when they went to open the refrigerator, someone had locked the damn thing and they couldn't get it open. Well, that's the charm of live broadcast, whether it's TV or radio. Yes, it is a little rough around the edges, but that's what makes it appealing. People love it because it's unique and amusing.

My program, *Coast to Coast*, is a little rough. I deliberately keep my show from being polished, like, say, Rush Limbaugh's program. Limbaugh's program is well planned and choreographed, and the call screeners are well seasoned at selecting callers; this gives the show a polished and professional effect. His show is also predictable, far from spontaneous. Now, I suppose, because I have been doing *Coast to Coast* for so long, I may make my show sound polished. But the spontaneity of unscreened callers keeps the edge.

The Secret's in the Preparation

It's not unusual when things go wrong on my show, or when things get crazy, or when news breaks. I'll stop everything to address what's going on, right then and there. Also, just so that I am not taken totally by surprise by what happens in the world, and to address the many varied topics callers wish to discuss, I do my homework. I prepare up to five hours every day, reading newspapers, staying tuned to CNN, monitoring the on-line news services, reading my many, many faxes I get from everywhere, night and day, reading my bags of mail, and so on.

I believe that as a talk show host, you cannot get away with being unprepared. If you think you can, your audience will eat you alive. I know that there have been a couple of times in the past when, either because of illness or some personal situation, I was not prepared for a show. Well, you only need to do that once to realize you cannot get away with it. These days, if something gets in the way of my efforts to be prepared, I will not go on the air. I would rather air a pre-recorded show or have someone substitute for me. But, normally, I will be prepared, very prepared. I must. I cannot and will not bluff my listeners.

As far as I'm concerned, too many talk show hosts get away with murder; they do their programs with either little or no preparation.

I have heard some hosts who are so ill prepared, the listeners have to give the host the latest news. It's ridiculous. How can you talk with someone who does not know what you're talking about? This does not make for good dialogue, it probably ought to be embarrassing for the host, and really I think it defeats the purpose of a talk show.

Look for Controversy

I want to know in general what has gone on during the day, and I make a special effort to learn what is controversial. In short, I look for what people probably want to talk about. I have cultivated the capacity to recognize right away what will be fluff, and not talk-worthy, and what will be of interest and something definitely worth talking about. I have learned to identify controversy and a good story. All I need to do is watch a TV broadcast, or read the paper, and I will know what is good to talk about.

For example, if, say, a tragic airplane accident occurs, and many people die because of an aviation mishap, this is clearly news and very horrible, but is it something people will want to talk about? No. There is nothing left to talk about, other than that it was horrible. The accident occurred because of pilot error, say, and that's that. But what if the plane crashed because a bomb exploded aboard? That's news and something definitely worth talking about on my program. Why? Because you can have a discussion about, for example, who would blow up the airplane? This is a story, a controversy, something with talk value. Suppose there is another airplane crash, only this time the crash is the result of a worn part on the aircraft. This crash also does not have much talk value. No one deliberately installed a worn part, so we can only accept this as a tragedy and that's all there is to it. I know this may sound strange, but it is something I have discovered over the years about the talk value of various news stories.

The Right Questions

Another reason I think *Coast to Coast* is so popular is that I have learned to ask the right questions. If I cannot find a relevant question as it relates to a news story, then I will not use the story. The story, then, has no talk value. This is not to say the story is not good material for a news broadcast because it is. But talk radio is a forum for talk and one must have something to talk about for talk radio to work. This is a tip I give nearly every up and coming talk show host I get the opportunity to talk to. The challenge is to find interest, entertainment, and some value in a story to appeal to listeners.

Sincerity

I also think *Coast to Coast* is so popular because I am sincere to my listeners. God help a talk show host dealing with one controversy after another and not expressing sincere feelings or views about those controversies. God help such a host because they will be caught in their own web of insincerity. Listeners know when you're putting them on. You might get away with being disingenuous for one or two shows, maybe even over the course of a week of shows, but you will not be able to keep this up month after month, year after year. It is better to keep things simple. I tell the truth; that's what I do. I tell my listeners what I feel. Then I can rest easy, because chances are that I will still hold the same view on a topic several months from now, maybe even several years from now. In other words, I'll be consistent because I say exactly how I feel.

I genuinely enjoy interacting honestly and openly with my callers. I love listening to what they have to say about a given topic, and I love telling them just what I feel about that topic. And apparently, my listeners must enjoy talking to me; the caller lines are always lit up.

Guests

I don't *need* to have guests on *Coast to Coast* all the time because I don't have to worry about filling time; there is plenty to talk about and I know my listeners enjoy listening and talking to *me*. However, my show is a success because the guests that I do have on are good, and I pick and choose them very, very carefully. I know what my listeners are interested in, and I can talk about what interests them, and when I have guests, my guests will talk about what interests my listeners. There seems to be a tendency by talk show hosts around the country who feel as though they have to fill in time, so they often do so by having guests. I don't think this is necessary. If there is a really interesting guest who I have been dying to interview, and who I am sure my listeners will love, I'll get that guest on my show. I will have anyone on who is interesting or contemporary.

So, there are a few thoughts on why I think my show and I have succeeded. And as the old adage goes, if it ain't broke, don't fix it. If you are successful at something, just keep doing the same thing and you can perpetuate success, and that's exactly what I plan on doing as long as I can.

Coast to Coast AM Grows...Fast!!

Coast to Coast is growing very, very quickly. I am awed and amazed at the show's growth. And I must admit, even though I am excited and happy over all this growth, I get rather nervous and even scared about it, too. For example, on the night I was to air for the first time on our new Los Angeles affiliate (at the time, KMPC, now KABC), I was all too aware that this area is the second largest radio market in the country (New York is number one). Well, as hard as I tried not to let this make me nervous, I ended up succumbing to a very intense anxiety attack; I sweat bullets through that first airing. As much as I tried to persuade myself of my confidence, I still experienced this in all the other major markets we broke into in the last few years, like Boston and New York City.

What may seem strange to everyone else is that I would ever get nervous at this point in my career. I have been in radio for more than 30 years, and I have known for a long time that, at any given moment, millions are listening to me. Still, I do get nervous, very, very nervous at all this growth. It's hard to believe sometimes, but I am slowly accepting the idea. I suppose the only way I can deal with all this is by not thinking about how many people are listening to me, punching the next blinking light on my phone lines, and taking each caller one at a time. That's when I am at my best. I'm also at my best when I get wrapped up in a story. There is a story that catches everyone's thinking and I get into it. Then everyone gets into it. It's fun, it's exciting, and it's entertaining.

Of course, along with the growth of *Coast to Coast*, my popularity has grown. The phones are jammed every night, the fax reels off hundreds of faxes night and day, and I continually receive US Postal tubs and bags of mail, as well as a packed e-mail box; all this activity has elevated dramatically. Recent Arbitron surveys revealed that in many markets across the country, there are certain segments of time during the course of my program when I capture 90% of the listeners in those markets. I look at the surveys and just find it hard to believe so many people choose to listen to me over any other programming that exists in their market.

The Media

I would not say that the media has come to accept as a whole the kinds of things I talk about on my shows. I am still out on the edge. As far as still being pigeon-holed, like, oh, Art Bell, aliens and UFOs, yes I am. But that's fine. I don't care. I will take the labels, however they want to put it. My listeners know better. Of course I do that stuff, but I do a lot more, as anyone who listens to my show knows. You can't yet call it mainstream, and thus you cannot expect the mainstream media to welcome me with open arms, but there is definitely a growing interest in the kinds of issues I talk about on my shows. In terms of actual treatment by the media, I have generally been treated fairly and my privacy has generally been respected, with only a few exceptions.

The newspapers have given me more attention recently, and they have been generally very favorable in their reviews and coverage of me and of my show. The only trouble with the articles is that the photos of me are usually not very good. Otherwise, I just take this type of exposure in stride.

Television

The one law I have laid down is that I am extremely reluctant when it comes to television, and I almost never accept offers to appear on television. Despite my reputation for this, I am still approached by TV people. I have turned down many interviews, even some opportunities to appear on some rather prominent TV shows. My objection to television is that it is very structured. You are only allowed to speak in sound bites: itty bitty fragments of time that really don't give you enough time to say anything. Moreover, you are forced to compete with other people to get a sound bite or two in during an interview. I don't believe this can be very interesting and I don't think it can be very fun.

The other objection I have to television is that I believe it will give me fame and recognition that can interfere with my desire to maintain a private life. As I said earlier, I must maintain my private life because it is the only way I will be able to survive the pressures of doing a popular show such as mine, day in and day out. The trouble with doing a television interview, say on-site, is that the television people come in to my home dragging cameras and lights that blow circuit breakers, etc. They change everything for their own benefit and I have had enough of that. I need my privacy.

People have asked me if I would ever consider a pilot, something like Rush Limbaugh's television show. I would say that I am not open to that at this point. Television is not something I look at in terms of my moving up. In other words, radio is not my

184

trampoline or launching pad to a career in television. I am very satisfied with all that I have achieved over the years and I feel that I can do without television. I like radio because it is right there, it's not contrived or rehearsed. When I do my shows, I savor the uncertainty of each call and each show. You can't have that in television.

So I suppose that I accept my popularity as part of what I do; however, I am wary of the effect my popularity will have on my private life. This is something I will try my best to preserve, no matter how big the show gets. I should say, of course, that I am grateful for how the show has grown and I am grateful for how people have come to appreciate what I do.

Dark Skies

Although I continue to be reluctant about television, I was approached by NBC producer, Bryce Zabel about appearing on their (unfortunately now defunct) television show, *Dark Skies*. Television is hectic, rehearsed and agonizingly slow, and my experience at NBC validated everything I have thought about television. I went to Los Angeles, and spent eight hours, including makeup, producing a 2 ½ minute spot to air. Don't ask me exactly why I agreed to do this. Maybe I figured that since there was an actual script, I would know exactly what I was going to do and how it was going to turn out when it aired.

As far as the actual experience, I was nervous beforehand, just like before my radio show. I did have a nice long talk with character actor J.T. Walsh, and he relaxed me. He was a very nice guy and I admired him. Everyone was generally friendly and low-key, but then they did it every day of their lives.

Bryce Zabel asked me later to be in a second episode where I would have been a co-star. I declined, not only because it was so much trouble and effort to do, but because of the regulations imposed on me by the Screen Actors Guild (SAG). For the first appearance on television or in the movies, they let you get away with not joining and paying them their dues. But for the second, there is no choice. I would have been paid for the role, but it would have been more money to have to join SAG than I would have made with the part.

I am going to be in a movie, however; again, I think I feel more certain about the outcome of this type of filming, plus I will probably have a voice role. So that doesn't bother me as much since I do that every night. This movie, called *Chupacabra*, will be distributed in theaters nationwide and it will start shooting in the next six months.

Media Awards

In my industry, the two greatest compliments you can receive as a talk show host are the number of people who want to listen to you and the praise of your industry peers. After all, this is a very competitive field. People can easily just turn the dial and move on to another station or show. Colleagues can just as easily lavish their approval upon someone else. So it was with great pleasure that I received a call from Alan Corbeth to inform me that I had been picked as Best Male Talk Show Host of 1997 by the very prestigious industry magazine, *Talkers*. Interestingly, Joy Browne, the up and coming radio relationships expert won Best Female Talk Show Host of 1997. There was also a very flattering article about me published in *Talkers*.

Ramona and I flew down to Los Angeles June 20, 1997, and met Bob and Sue Crane, Alan and Leona Corbeth, Jennifer Osborn and Werner Riefling, my publisher after our limousine ride from LAX at the hotel where the event was being held. Sitting at a circular table near the stage, I picked my way nervously through a lunch consisting of some odd chicken dish, a salad made of weeds and a dessert no one had the courage to touch. Not that it would have mattered since I was so busy agonizing over what I would say and how I would perform on stage.

As my award was announced, my stomach did a little flip flop and I exhaled with the relief of someone who had finally finished at the dentist. All I wanted was to get this over with. In front of the audience of my peers, I kept it brief. "I have taken a different path than many of my talk radio peers. For those of you who have followed me in that direction, thank you. And thank you for this recognition." Then I fled.

After the ceremony there was much photo taking and handshaking. Well-known names of the radio world whirled around me: Michael Reagan, Jim Bohanon, Michael Jackson, Casey Kasem. Returning with my entourage to the penthouse suite that Bob Crane had rented, we opened a bottle of champagne out on the deck. Enthralled, we all watched as the cork hurtled down to the street below and plonked a man standing below squarely on the head. Whoops! We all rushed back into the room, horrified. Later on, when the coast was clear, I constructed a couple of paper airplanes and launched them. The wind carried the slim craft for a few minutes through a canyon of buildings out on the Avenue of the Stars.

An early dinner and Ramona and I were whisked by limo back to the airport so I could do *Dreamland* the next day. Sometime later in the year, I learned that I had been nominated for yet another prestigious award, the Marconi. In that case, the ceremonies were being held in New Orleans, Louisiana and it was simply not possible for me to attend. But any attention of this nature is always a great compliment to me and I am very appreciative. Considering that I started so many years ago as a boy with my HAM radio equipment in my bedroom and am now, as an adult, receiving awards just for doing what I love, I feel pretty lucky.

The Toughest Stories

The toughest shows are the ones with guests. The easiest shows are open line shows where I get to relax somewhat. The very toughest shows are the ones where I have debates and two people are in contention. From the talk show host's point of view, that's really tough because I have to sit there and listen to every single word very carefully. And I am listening for many things at once.

I'm listening for content, fairness, legal problems, etc. So it's very draining.

But my shows can also be tough mentally and sometimes even emotionally as a result of the subject matter. One of the toughest stories I have covered on *Coast to Coast AM* was the Persian Gulf War. Looking back on it with 20/20 hindsight, you can say it was not much of a war. After all, we certainly did prevail easily in dealing with the Iraqis. At the time, however, we did not really know what we were facing. The situation was ominous. We thought we were facing hundreds of thousands of Iraqi troops prepared to die for their invasion of Kuwait, and the potential invasion of Saudi Arabia, and the taking over of the oil fields. We faced real fears of possible chemical or nuclear confrontation. The people who went over there were as brave as anyone who ever went to war with all the uncertainties at that time. The specter was frightening.

I remember when news got out that thousands of body bags were ordered by the Pentagon in anticipation of many, many casualties. We were all unsure about this situation, and the buildup to it went on and on. And on a nightly basis, this pretty much became the only topic I talked about and the only topic my listeners wanted to talk about. In hindsight it is easy to say we just rolled over the Iraqis. Of course, this was mostly because of the genius of Norman Schwartzkopf and Colin Powell, who planned and executed very well. I even must give credit to George Bush for having the presence of mind to do what needed to be done in the Middle East and then to let the military do their job without interference on his part. At the time, though, I must say I was scared. I was scared for America and I was scared for the men and women who were going over to the Persian Gulf.

There were about half a million American men and women who were sent to the Persian Gulf. Every night, for a good couple of months, my listeners and I argued about whether our troops should be over there and the possible consequences of not going over there. We talked about Saddam Hussein. We discussed the possibilities of American casualties. We also discussed the consequences if Iraq was permitted to continue unchecked. I believe Saddam Hussein would have moved further and eventually taken over the Saudi oil fields.

War is always a hard decision to make, whether or not it's worth it. This was definitely one of the harder stories I ever covered. Any time you talk about American flesh and blood going into harm's way, it is a very hard story. And at this writing, I'm afraid the discussions will probably be much the same with regard to the war going on in the Balkans and the genocide which is continuing, and whether or not the US should be involved.

Oklahoma City

The Oklahoma City bombing was a very tough story to cover. I recall the day the bomb went off. I was doing an interview with a radio station in Missouri and keeping my eye on CNN (which I sometimes show closed captioned) while I was on the phone. In the interview, I was discussing *Coast to Coast AM*, responding to questions about what I talk about on the air and so forth. As I was doing the interview, I looked over at the screen and saw this building that looked as though an atomic bomb had just gone off somewhere nearby, blowing about half the building away. At that moment, I interrupted the interview and addressed the listeners of this Missouri radio station, "Well, folks, I think we have a very serious story developing right now in Oklahoma City." Little did I know how serious it was.

That night I went on the air, but I had very few facts about what went on in Oklahoma City, except that the building had blown up. We had no idea who did it; there was only speculation, and the whole thing was running wild. I was on the air in Oklahoma City, so I was able to talk to the people there. This may or may not have been an advantage; I'm not sure. But these people, and the people of America, were in deep shock. I was one of them. I said to everyone then, and for several succeeding nights, "Let us pray that this was done by some foreign force."

189

Early on, authorities believed that this was some Middle Eastern terrorism. I was really hoping that this was the case because, if so, you have an enemy that you can identify. In the back of my mind, however, I feared that this tragedy was brought on by Americans. I knew that the bombing had occurred on the anniversary of the Waco tragedy with the Branch Davidians, when ATF agents stormed their compound in Waco, Texas and killed the people there. I feared that the bombing of the federal building in Oklahoma City may have been committed by militia members in retaliation for the Waco tragedy. It is a known fact that there are well armed militant groups throughout this country that hate agents operating for the Alcohol Tobacco and Firearms agency of the federal government.

Of course, in the meantime, we learned that the Oklahoma bombing *was* motivated by the Waco tragedy. This fact scares the hell out of me. To me, this means this country is in bigger trouble than most people realize. This has the potential of resulting in some horrible incident in which Americans are pitted against each other. America should come to terms with itself and know the truth of what is happening in this country today, and unfortunately, the televised Waco congressional hearings did not yield much healing. People still believe that in some way the government mishandled the whole Waco incident. This to me suggests that Americans are growing cynical. But Americans must be aware that this country is going to ruin itself if the continued cynicism is not curtailed. A recent survey showed that three out of four Americans do not trust their government and frankly, I don't blame them, although things should not be this way. The danger of this should be apparent: as Americans fear their government more and more, their government fears those whom they govern more and more. The possibility for tragedy increases exponentially. And that's where we are right now in this country.

In short, we must televise and otherwise let the American people know the truth about what this government does. As things are hidden or covered up, and the truth is evaded, the people find out sooner or later, and this undermines their faith in those who run the country. It sets everyone up for tragedy. It unravels what this country's founding fathers intended in that great document the Constitution.

O.J. Simpson

Next on my list of tough stories would be the O.J. Simpson trial. I watched this trial religiously, right from the very beginning, with an almost morbid fascination. Frankly, from the start, I have felt O.J. Simpson murdered his ex-wife, Nicole Brown Simpson, and her friend, Ronald Goldman. I felt that he would be found guilty and convicted; perhaps the defense just seemed ineffective at the beginning. Then about halfway through the trial, I developed the opinion that the trial would end in a hung jury. I speculated that there would be enough reasonable doubt introduced, enough holes punched in the prosecution's case that it would be at the very least a hung jury. Towards the end of the trial, I developed the opinion that O.J. would be found *not guilty*. This is not to say that I changed my mind of his guilt, but that his defense attorneys had done such a good job that he would go free.

A message of "not guilty" in this case hurts the American justice system. This just creates another reason for Americans to raise the level of cynicism about the way things work in this country. Even during the trial, many people developed the opinion that O.J.'s attorneys were so good at their jobs, they were able to inject reasonable doubt. Which means, essentially, O.J. purchased for himself reasonable doubt in his defense. This has made many people feel that there is an imbalance in the justice system, that all you need is money to buy your way out of a crime, even murder. Of course, this is a reflection of a capitalistic country; the people with the gold rule. Even if the jury reached a verdict and Americans know the outcome of this trial, we may never know the truth about whether or not O.J. committed these murders.

Paula Jones & the Presidential Sex Scandals

Recently, of course, the whole Paula Jones story, which built into an enormous furor, died down with barely a quiet sizzle. On legal points, I believe the judge who dismissed the case was absolutely correct. You have got to either show a repetitive problem—that's the nature of sexual misconduct, that it occurs more than once or that someone presses themselves on you after you have said no—or you have to show damage. And if you look at the record, she was actually promoted; she wasn't held back or squashed, so no damage.

Personally I believe that unless they can prove suborning to perjury or a crime, they have absolutely nothing. When Clinton was elected, I thought he would be death on a stick for America, but he has not been. In fact, in a lot of ways, America is growing up and realizing that presidents are no different from factory workers. I don't frankly care what Clinton does in his private life unless he breaks the law. It has yet to be seen whether he did and if he did then he's in trouble. Based on what we know so far, it's only 'he said, they said,' and that is not going to get a president impeached.

Ironically enough, the more women that come out, the higher the popularity has gone up, the higher the approval rating has gone. That's a comment on contemporary society and that's a comment on the fact that employment is high, interest rates are low, the market is breaking new highs every day and they're not going to let Clinton's wandering hands screw up the economy.

The presidential sex scandals have been tough because of the pressure on me to cover them the way the rest of the media was covering them and I didn't want to. And I didn't. In other words, the talk radio industry concentrated very heavily on the sex aspect of the whole thing, when the real questions were legal questions about supporting perjury and perjury itself. Those are the very serious questions and the actual sex angle I guess is interesting or irresistible for most talk show hosts. But I successfully resisted it and I think the rest of the country did as well. The talk show hosts thought it was a huge deal and the country, if you read the polls, obviously did not. When something like this comes along, you have to decide how you feel about it and how you're going to handle it.

The Best & Worst Callers

On *Coast to Coast AM*, I take calls on my show for the better part of five hours every night, five nights a week. I have been doing this now for about six years. That's an awful lot of calls. And up till about three years ago, I still had best and worst callers. Today I would say that the show has grown to the point where it's very difficult to have a regular call base; you just don't have it. It's just that there are too many people and no single person is able to get through that many times to become a known presence on the program.

Now I have favorite types of callers and they're generally people that are either entertaining or really bizarre. I mean, I love bizarre calls. I nurture them. I open subject-specific lines to encourage weirdness. For instance, one night I opened a special government agent line. It was really funny and serious at the same time. So the show has changed to the degree that it is so much bigger that no single person gets through frequently. People who are at the extremes are very important to the show. The best callers add spice to the show and drive it through the nighttime.

The worst callers are those who really have nothing to say. And they seem to be calling just to hear their own voices on the radio. But because I don't screen calls, I am bound to get these types of calls. I get everything. If I get a caller whose intellectual contribution is going to be nothing, I try to take the call and convert it into entertainment or maybe even information. Tedium, boredom and uninteresting people will not hold an audience. So I always try to make things interesting, informative, and entertaining whether I am talking to the best callers or the worst callers, and the many that are in between. But I believe this is where the skill of handling callers enters the show. A good talk show host will know how to turn a boring or empty call into at least a fairly entertaining call.

I know that there are talk show hosts who are not even interested in what they are doing. They just want to get through their day and get home. They are not concerned about the quality of the show, whether or not it is interesting or informative. They will just answer the next caller and will most likely let someone boring or uninteresting drone on and on. It won't take long before many listeners grow weary of this and stop listening. This is why many radio talk shows don't succeed. The talk show host does not do their homework, they do not take an interest in the topics discussed, and they don't know how to handle callers, the good, the bad, or the in-between, and to make the show interesting.

For years I did have a favorite caller, who I refer to as a conservative curmudgeon who lived in Mount Shasta, California, but who since passed away. I thoroughly enjoyed talking to this caller on the air, and I believe many listeners enjoyed listening to this caller, too. And callers have come and gone over the years. I have had many regular liberal callers come and go, and I have had many regular conservative callers come and go. People tend to do that with radio. Occasionally you lose a good caller, but then you get a good caller. It's all part of the business. Now that the show has grown like it has, I am glad that I went through a period where I did have regular callers.

The Quickening

Of the many topics I bring up on *Coast to Coast AM*, one of the most important and serious is something I call the Quickening. In all the years I have been on the air with my radio program, I have seen things begin to accelerate in nearly every aspect of American life. After several years of taking note of this accelerated trend (accelerated in mostly a negative way), I finally summed it up one night on the air and just called everything that was going on 'the Quickening.' I have talked about the Quickening for the last eleven years on the air, and my book, *The Quickening*, was the most natural result of all that. Here are a few of the things that I am seeing in the country today.

Society

Socially, America is definitely in a rapidly escalating crisis. One example of this would be the riots in Los Angeles that occurred after the Rodney King verdict: the unbelievable violence, the defiance against authority, the blatant looting, and so on. The social crisis is also exemplified by the increased cheapening of life in America. Gangs are on the rise comprised of people who think nothing of murdering people just to have the experience of killing someone. This is a phenomenon that never really existed before in this country. It is a reflection of the way people are being raised in this country. Too many people are growing up in broken families and have not been given any sense of value, of their own or of others. Grown in its place is instead a definite lack of self-respect and the basic respect of the lives of other people.

Not too many years ago, criminals would rob someone and usually not kill them. These days, however, it is a documented fact that criminals will rob people and kill them just for the fun of it. In fact, murder has steadily risen over the last few years with no diminishing numbers in sight. There was a time in this country when the greatest likelihood of being murdered was by someone you knew: a spouse, a fellow employee, a neighbor, etc. Someone who may have had a grudge against you, or whatever, but there were clear motives for murder. Now, the statistics indicate that you are more likely to be murdered by a complete stranger for no real motive.

The innocence that America had back in the 1950s has been long lost. As I said in *The Quickening*, many of us have a hard time seeing that everything around us is *not* okay. People are starving in countries far away from us, but women are also being raped and murdered in the house next door. We complacently watch violence on television and in movies, but want our children to be protected from such horrors as drugs, alcohol and sex at young age. Society and societal ills have progressed at such a rapid rate and along such negative trends that most of the issues that need to be addressed are out of human control. I just get frustrated because I just see people not thinking about things that need to be thought about more carefully. And most issues have to be addressed, when they can, at an individual level.

Weather Patterns

More evidence of the Quickening includes the dramatically changing weather patterns; there is more violent weather than ever before. Earthquakes, hurricanes, and other acts of nature are happening with increasing frequency; more of everything which seems to have a detrimental effect on the people of this country seems to be accelerating. And these things seem to be coming at a faster pace. People everywhere are beginning to feel the hair stand up on the back of their necks as if they realize something is about to happen, perhaps some sort of judgment. I also feel something is about to happen and all these accelerated things seem to point to the same conclusion.

I find it particularly amusing, in the area of weather for one example, that I am called paranoid and crazy. The truth is that what is weird tonight, on my show, is headlines on *The Washington Post* in a few months from now. I was talking about El Niño and the weather changes we're going to face a year ago, and I was a nut then. Now I'm getting called a prophet. This is really amusing to me.

Am I a Prophet?

Now, I know there are a lot of my listeners who translate my observations and my use of the expression the Quickening into something biblical. And who am I to say it does not translate into something biblical? Nonetheless, I am not on the air telling anyone that it does. I am also not on the air telling people that Armageddon is just around the corner, or that these days in which

196

we live are the final days of life on earth. I really have no idea about any of that. I also don't claim to predict future events. But I don't think you have to be a rocket scientist to easily come to conclusions about where we are headed. All I have done is make a pragmatic observation of the acceleration of events in every category of life, and collectively called it the Quickening. I don't want it to mean 'the end.' I want to see, as Paul Harvey would say, 'the rest of the story.'

The Soul of America

One night, several years ago, I did a program on the soul of America. And this program received more of a response than nearly any program I have ever done. Before then, I never thought of or considered that a country has a soul. This was a new concept I introduced at the time. Of course, in the very strictest sense, I suppose we don't really have a soul. But metaphorically, our country certainly does have a soul. America is a state of mind. America still is an extension of what our founding fathers envisioned it to be in the document they created: the wonderful Constitution of America. So that *is* our soul.

Anyway, after defining our soul, I asked my listeners: "Is our soul wounded? Have we lost our soul as a nation?" I guess it really has not died because the spark of life in our collective chest is still alive. But our soul *is* wounded. It is wounded by all the elements of the Quickening (i.e., the economic decline, the social upheaval, the political corruption, the natural disasters, etc.). Our soul is wounded by fallen heroes (the O.J. Simpsons and others like him), so many role models who have been revealed to have clay feet. Our soul has been wounded and hurt by the institutions that have been shaken by contemporary events. Our national soul has definitely been wounded.

The next question I posed, and I continue to pose: "Is this wound of our national soul a fatal wound?" From my perspective, I prefer not to see the half-*empty* glass of water, but half *full*. Nonetheless, I do think that this may very well be a fatal wound.

And it may be that America will in effect have to crash and burn. However, if this should happen, I can only hope that America can still rise from the ashes like a phoenix and become strong again. I can only hope that under those conditions, America can still be a representative republic and land of the relatively free.

And Where Do We Go From Here?

I really don't like being negative about America. I admit, it may be my age showing. But I would rather think that it is my years of experience in dealing directly with America's people from my very unique position as a radio talk show host. The advantage of my position is that I can see the trends and I can be realistic about the way I think the world is going. The level of cynicism and distrust has never been higher. We may have passed the social point of no return. I don't know, I am still puzzling this one out myself, but I strongly sense we are on the verge of something that does not look very good. Our soul is certainly wounded and I don't know what I should be praying for. Should I pray for a healing process to begin? Whether it can I'm not even sure. Or should I pray for a quick end to an abysmal situation? And then, after such a culmination, should I hope for the country to go on to whatever is next?

I would say that I see civilization at a crossroads and I believe that unless things change or humans change things drastically, we are not in for a bright, happy future. Just wanting to believe that things are 'not really that bad' is not going to make it so. I have my eyes open and I think people would be a lot better off doing the same.

Some Interesting Shows

There are a number of memorable topics or stories that I have aired over the years which I personally and many of my listeners seemed to take a special interest in, or just found entertaining and thought provoking. I'll share several of these stories here.

Black Box

I am a person who likes to study human nature. One time I did an entire show — I think this might have come from a Twilight Zone episode — that was designed to reveal something about everyone who called. The hypothesis: you are given a black box. On the black box, there is a single button. Now, in order to get one million dollars in good hard cash, all you need to do is push the button. But, when and if you do, somewhere, somebody is going to drop dead immediately. Then they will take the box away and that's it. You have your million dollars. You have no idea who you killed or how they died. The reactions on both an emotional and moral level are fascinating. This is another example of a show that I will do that may have nothing to do with contemporary issues at all. But I do shows like that because I love seeing how people react and I love talking to people about things like that.

Audio Animals

One night I went to go on the air and there was no audio. The arrangement I have is that my studio is in one room and in the adjacent room I have the up-link transmitter. That means that there had to be wiring put underneath the house in order to traverse the audio between these two rooms. Therefore, the technical crew from CBC and I started troubleshooting equipment like crazy. We checked my studio, the audio processing equipment and even the up-link equipment, and everything was fine.

Finally, out of frustration, I pulled on the wire that connected my studio equipment and the audio between these two rooms. I pulled and pulled and pulled until it came out of the floor cut in half. I mean, it was cut in half as cleanly as if you had taken a pair of scissors and just chopped right through it. Some animal, I don't know what, under the house, had munched through my cord. I only got on the air that night by running an emergency cord from one room to the other.

I was so angry that after that, I took a .22 rifle and went under my house, hunting for this mysterious critter with a taste for metal and rubber. Of course, despite making this into a morning ritual for a while, I never did see him or figure out what it was. To this day, I do not run the wiring underneath the house so that cannot ever happen again!

What Would You Do If...?

I prefer science fiction that is based on science *fact*; in other words, science fiction that is based on some reasonably predictable future that doesn't go too far afield. I don't like reading books about "Captain Zolith" from the "Starship such and such" in the "Zada Riticuli" system, for instance. Therefore, I tend to especially enjoy covering stories such as the discovery and implications of the Hale-Bopp comet.

Originally, it was reported in the Sunday *London Telegraph*. This comet appeared to have crept into our solar system from the depths of space, fueling inevitable concern for the end of the world. In the beginning, because of the relative brightness of this comet, it was reported to be as large as 1,000 miles across. So, one night on *Coast to Coast*, I went on the air and asked the loaded question. What if a comet, maybe this one or another one, was headed toward Earth and we only had a few weeks, a few months, or even a few years left, but we knew that the world was going to end?

There were a number of interesting responses to this. Some people, perhaps inevitably, said, well, Art, I would go home and I would be with my family. With that in mind, when I asked everyone, "What will everyone else do?" the answer was that there would be anarchy. What is the real answer? Would everyone go and quietly contemplate their last minutes or would it suddenly be a world of chaos and panic? I don't know the answer. Do you?

Whale Blubber

I get lots of interesting stories from my listeners. Normally, I try to have a story confirmed, especially if it sounds interesting, but almost hard to believe. Anyway, the whale blubber story was something that came to me as a fax called "The Far Side Comes to

Life in Oregon" — and it is an account of the stupidity of the Oregon State Highway Division.

The man who faxed me the story said he had videotaped the story that aired on a local TV news broadcast. Apparently, a 45-foot, eight-ton dead whale had washed up on the beach. For some reason, the Oregon State Highway Division was given the responsibility to remove the dead carcass. After considering several ways of achieving this, the highway engineers decided that the most expedient means to remove the whale was to blow the thing up with a half-ton of dynamite, and leave the small pieces that remained for the seagulls. So, with that in mind, they moved the spectators up the beach some distance, put a half-ton of dynamite next to whale carcass, and set the thing off.

The moment the whale was detonated, there was a glorious cloud of smoke and fire as the huge carcass disappeared. The spectators cheered and whistled and carried on, perhaps in admiration of this feat undertaken with such adeptness by the Oregon State Highway Division. That is, until a huge thud was heard, as a giant piece of whale blubber crushed the roof of a car not too far off. This was almost immediately followed by a shower of whale blubber falling everywhere, hitting and splatting on everything, including the video camera lens that was smeared with the unseemly substance. After the shower settled, one could see several chunks of whale blubber the size of condominium units that landed on the beach. There were no sea gulls in sight and all the people had scurried off, seeking shelter.

The man who sent the fax indicated that the video of this event was something he and his friends enjoyed watching over and over again. He said that it was especially good entertainment at parties. I wondered how much it cost in tax dollars to finally clean up the mess. Nonetheless, this was a very funny story. Throughout that show, listeners called in suggesting alternatives that the Oregon State Highway Division may have used to clean up the whale.

Halloween

Just about every Halloween I have a special show that features scary ghost stories, stories about the paranormal, or anything else which may scare the bejeezus out of my listeners. And most of the time, I know that people do get scared listening to that show. In fact, since I know some of the stories are invariably frightening, I even give my listeners fair warning so they can turn my program off to avoid getting scared.

Anyway, here is a true ghost story that I aired and which has even scared me. I'll print the story here more or less as I received it via fax.

"I was an Eastern Orthodox Priest for many years, and in that time I have witnessed many interesting if not frightening things. This is one that I would like to relate to you.

"In 1974, a close friend of mine lost her father. He had been very popular during the '40s as a singer and guitar player on the radio. He and his wife had been divorced for many years at the time of his death. He lived alone and died of a heart attack while sleeping in his bed. It was three days before his body was discovered. About a week after the funeral, his ex-wife moved back into the house he had lived and died in.

"Two months after his death, I received a phone call from my friend, asking me if I could come over to her mother's house. Apparently, her mother was starting to act a little strange and she was concerned. When I got there, the three of us sat down and my friend's mother told me this story. She said she was convinced she was going crazy. She said that about two weeks earlier, she woke up in the middle of the night to the singing of her dead ex-husband. She walked into the front room and he was sitting in the rocking chair, smiling at her. She went back into the bedroom and spent the rest of the night with no more sleep.

"She then told me that after that encounter with her dead ex-husband, she would be sitting in the front room, and for no reason, it would feel like someone was grabbing or pinching her legs. After this strange sort of attack, she complained that welts would appear

202

on her legs. Also, she would continue to hear her dead ex-husband singing every night.

"I told her that I didn't think she was going crazy and (having had some experience with exorcism), I asked her if she would feel better if I went through the house and blessed it. She said it would make her feel better. I took out a small bottle of Holy Water, and proceeded to go through the house room by room starting with the basement. Everything went fine. I saved the bedroom for last. Upon entering the bedroom, there was a noticeable temperature difference; it was very cold and you could see your breath, like walking into a refrigerator. The mother stood in the doorway, and as I threw Holy Water around the room, the mother was thrown backwards, out of the doorway and into the hallway wall. When I asked her what was wrong, she said that something had hit her in the legs, like someone was trying to push her out of the way. I was a little skeptical until she pulled up her pant legs, and I could clearly see new, large red welts on both legs, just above each knee.

"I'm not sure exactly what went on in that house, but I do know there was something, and after I blessed the house, there were no further encounters with the dead ex-husband or any other physical manifestation."

Heaven's Gate

One of the strangest stories I have encountered recently was the swirling chaos of Heaven's Gate. The story went something like this: amateur astronomer Chuck Shramek had appeared on my show one night in November, 1996, alleging that there was an unusual "companion object" following the comet Hale-Bopp. As if this was not enough cause for bewilderment, excitement and as always, skepticism, Courtney Brown stepped into the situation later that month. He suggested that, based on several of his remote viewers from his own Farsight Institute, the object was "under intelligent control."

Furthermore, Courtney claimed that he had a photograph, given to him by an alleged university astronomy professor, revealing the object as an alien craft, from which radio signals were emitting. This revelation practically blew away my disbelieving side.

Courtney documented the claims he was making by providing a copy of the photograph to both Whitley Strieber and myself, with only one condition—that we wait for a promised news conference from the owner of the photograph in which all details would be revealed before we posted it publicly. I agreed that as long as this news conference took place in a timely fashion, I would uphold my end of the agreement. Six long weeks went by with no word. I don't consider myself a particularly patient person, but in this case, I think I was more than fair. On January 14, 1997, I called Courtney and left a message on his answering machine that I intended to post the photo on the Internet the next day.

Courtney left a long message on my answering machine, begging me for over three minutes not to post the photo, cajoling from every angle he could think of—including my reputation as a radio host and the fact that I had given my word—to prevent me from displaying this photo. Nevertheless, as far as I was concerned, Courtney's time was up and the next day, January 15, 1997, the photo hit the Internet on my web site.

The response was immediate. An email from the University of Hawaii Institute for Astronomy asserted that the photo was a fake and that in fact they had had the same photo posted on their web site for the last year. The game was up. The comet's mysterious "companion" was nothing more than a digitally inserted hoax. Even Courtney's story of the rolls of film could not have been true; a spokesman from the UH Institute confirmed that these photos would have been taken and processed digitally, not with film.

I felt it would only be fair to allow Courtney to return to the show and have the opportunity to explain himself. When I asked him how this could have happened, his reply was that he had walked into a trap, and that he was obviously the victim of a "highly organized 'disinformation campaign.'" He was close-mouthed about the source of the photo and reluctant to turn over any kind of film rolls he might have possessed. To this day, the mystery remains unsolved.

Obviously I had gone over the allegation thoroughly, debunking it *long before* 39 people committed suicide in a mansion in San Diego on March 21, 1997. Despite the fact that these people acknowledged that there was no companion in their suicide note, the April 14, 1997 issue of *Time* called me "the man who spread the myth." In light of that and other articles with similar angles, I received a sudden shower of media attention in the wake of these suicides, attempting to link me to them, to make me responsible in some way, perhaps as a co-conspirator. I had almost daily visits from magazines, newspapers and sensational television shows that in the end only wanted to create an exaggeration out of an event that was already shocking in the first place. They were looking for someone to blame and found that at the very least, it was not Art Bell's fault.

Despite accusations to the contrary, I feel that I was simply doing my job, providing the public with a forum to listen to and evaluate various ideas. As I said, it's important to understand that the only person who ever said there was a spacecraft following Hale-Bopp was Courtney Brown. Obviously I wouldn't want anyone to kill themselves because of something I said or something that was on my show. Nor would I have ever intentionally created a panic on a nationally syndicated radio show that reaches and possibly influences millions of people daily.

I think these people were serious, maybe seriously misled, but serious. Personally, my reaction was to reflect on the act of suicide and the value of life. I could never commit suicide because I feel we are put here to live our life and if we cut it short we will end up repeating it until we have fulfilled our destiny. However, these people felt strongly enough about the path they had chosen that they were willing to sacrifice their lives for it. Whether their particular faith was misbegotten or not, we still have to see the bigger picture: that they had this strength of belief in a time in history when it is hard to know what to believe in.

One strange and unexpected side effect of the Heaven's Gate suicides was a sudden, exponential increase in new affiliates. At the time, there were a handful of affiliates that were not quite sold on the idea of carrying my show. Evidently, all the media interest I was receiving was enough to convince many of these stations that I was worth airing in their areas of the country. Nevertheless, while the Heaven's Gate incident did result in adding more affiliates, and thus listeners, the major growth for *Coast to Coast AM* took place well afterwards.

Fan Mail, Hate Mail, & Love Mail

I get many faxes and letters sent to me on a daily basis. Fortunately, the great majority of these are laudatory and complimentary. As a percentage, I would say about 90% of my faxes and letters are of the praising variety. These are obviously my fans and they want to express their appreciation of me and of my show. I have fans from all walks of life and experiences, young and old, and some of them are famous and have fans of their own. As an example, I learned some time ago that the actress, Doris Day, is one of my fans. Steve and Edie Gormet, Willie Nelson, Merle Haggard and Crystal Gayle are also fans. I immensely appreciate all my fans, no matter who they are. I must confess, however, that I only very occasionally read faxes or letters that praise me or my show. The reason I don't read many of these correspondences is that it seems self-serving to me if I read things that only tell me how great I am.

More frequently, I read the bad stuff. These are the faxes and mail from the people who hate me. Yes, I have people who hate me, but I have come to terms with that. These people who really *hate* my guts comprise about five to seven percent of the correspondences I get. It may sound strange, but I actually monitor how much hate mail I get. I even worry if I don't get very much hate mail because then I begin to think I'm doing something wrong. After all, given so many millions of listeners, and given the many

206

topics on which I freely offer my views, surely there will be at least a small percentage of people who will hate my guts because of what I say.

And if I don't get much of a hateful response, then I am not saying things that really make many waves at all. Which, from my standpoint, means I'm not doing my job. I am in the business of unearthing controversial topics to stir things up and to invoke interesting and entertaining talk radio. This does not mean I say stupid things that are intended to create controversy; I am not in the business of manufacturing controversy for my own benefit. Rather, I become knowledgeable about what goes on in the world, and bring the interesting, and very likely the controversial, to my show. Manufacturing controversy and finding it are two very different things.

The people who hate me really express themselves hatefully. I have had explosives sent in the mail to me. So far, none of them have detonated, thank God. I have had the nastiest and most virulent mail. Some people have charged me as being the very worst kind of Nazi. Some people think I am tyrannical and a dictator, which I am to some degree, but only to maintain control of my radio program so it works.

I also get love mail. There have been a number of instances in which ladies have fallen in love with me over the radio. This is entirely possible. I know that listeners form a bond with talk show hosts. I have always known about this and have always worried about this tendency for bonding. Often, this bond between listener and talk show host can be very, very strong, and I don't take it lightly; I definitely feel the responsibility of this bond. And every so often, a listener will yield to this bond and allow it to translate into love. In some cases, this may evolve into a passionate sort of love and is very real to the listener who has these feelings. Consequently, I have received love letters. Generally, I don't keep the love letters.

I remember one lady down in Arizona who used to send me very serious love letters. Often these letters were perfumed and would jump out at me in pink envelopes. These letters were mushy and sensual and sexual and so on. My wife got a hold of these letters. Eventually, when my wife finally could not stand it any longer, she sat down and wrote this lady a letter. I imagine it was probably the most blistering letter anyone has ever seen.

I guess it is like anything else, you have extremes in everything even in the correspondences you receive. You have those who love you on one end of the spectrum, and you have those who hate your guts and wish you would have an aneurysm and die on the other end of the spectrum, and you have everything in between. This is probably a good reflection of the variety of humanity out there to which my show is exposed.

The Show's Bumper Music

Sometimes people ask me about the music I use on the air. As I have already indicated, I spent about twenty years in rock music radio. And unlike many radio personalities, I am quite comfortable running my own board for my show and mixing the music the way it feels right to me. If I had a producer, I could never do that. I am the only one who knows what kind of mood I want to project. And because I do my own mixing, I have music that will suit just about any mood there is. In network radio, you need what is known as bumpers. Bumpers are prerecorded music tapes or even prerecorded audio announcements which create a seamless connection between the show and the local network stations for a commercial break or a news break, and then from the network station back to the show. This keeps the flow of sound moving, and it adds a seamless, professional touch.

For music bumpers, I have collected what I love. For example, Cusco is a German musical group that I love to play as my bumper music. I also like to use old rock and roll, using the "hook" part of the tune. When I say *hook* part, I mean it's that part that gets you hooked into the feelings that the music can evoke. Obviously this is a very subjective thing, but something that I believe I've been

208

very successful at because I will receive calls from the callers who are eager to find the music I use. They want to listen to the bumper music all the time. Cusco has had this effect and this has resulted in the sales of many albums for Cusco to my listeners. I use the same 30 to 50 tunes again and again because they work. The audience enjoys it and becomes accustomed to hearing it. It's part of the whole package I air on my show and has, to some extent, helped me succeed.

And Beyond. . .

Already *Coast to Coast AM* has expanded beyond the shores of this continent to places like Tahiti, the Virgin Islands, and into parts of South America. In addition, you can hear me worldwide on shortwave. So it seems that it will not be restrained, nor will every caller's need to be heard, to share his or her opinion with the rest of the listeners. And so, this dynamic program will stretch, coming more and more into its own. All this because of a fateful meeting between two people who loved radio more than life. But then, isn't that the best kind of destiny?

9

DREAMLAND

"Welcome to Dreamland, a program dedicated to an examination of areas of the human experience not easily or neatly put in a box, things seen at the edge of vision, awakening a part of the mind as yet not mapped and yet things every bit as real as the air we breathe but don't see. This is Dreamland."

Dreamland is a program that is close to my heart. Before doing *Dreamland*, I did a radio program called *Area 2000* broadcasting from KDWN in Las Vegas. We wanted the show to deal with issues that arose as we headed toward the turn of the century, or as I call it, the millennium, and that's how we came up with the name. *Area 2000* dealt with very much the same topics that I deal with on *Dreamland*, with very much the same format. The show was funded by an organization that was very interested in having these issues looked at seriously. After I moved to Pahrump and went to work for Chancellor Broadcasting to do *Coast to CoastAM*, *Area 2000* ended. There was a great hue and cry and I also was not happy that the show had ended.

After I had been doing *Coast to Coast* for a while, I felt that there was a void which needed filling. I knew that I missed doing *Area 2000*. After being bothered by this for some time, I finally called Alan Corbeth and told him how I felt. Alan, being open-minded and just a good businessman, agreed to help me get a new show going based on *Area 2000*. So was born the idea of *Dreamland*. Even though I work five days, I don't mind working a sixth day because it is a labor of absolute love.

Area 51

As I have already indicated, I live in Pahrump. And it just so happens that out in the middle of the Nevada desert, within a short drive north of Pahrump, there is a rather controversial and significant government zone called Area 51. Area 51 is often referred to as *Dreamland*. The name is derived from the strange activities that occur in this government-sanctioned area. The pilots that are selected call this area *Dreamland* because they are able to fly airplanes that are generations ahead of anything else that is being flown today. It has been known for many years that the government uses Area 51 as a place to test unusual aircraft, perhaps the engineering feats of the figments of some scientist's imagination or possibly the technical dreams of some aeronautical wizard.

Furthermore, rumors have it that the government has also obtained and housed in *Dreamland* aircraft from somewhere out of this world. Not only are some of these aircraft reported to resemble flying disks or saucers, but there have also been many reported sightings of such craft in *Dreamland*. Being so physically close to this area and dealing with topics that relate to it, I decided the most natural name for my new program would be *Dreamland*.

At first, there were some people who thought the name *Dreamland* was not a good idea. After all, they claimed such a name might actually undermine the credibility of the various scientists, the academics, the authors, the various professionals, and many others who were guests on my show. Perhaps people would not find the name of the show serious enough, especially when so many people even question the legitimacy of the topics in the first place.

After a while, a funny thing happened. I began getting faxes and phone calls from listeners who exclaimed, "What a brilliant name! It absolutely fits what you're doing." People have fallen in love with the program, which presently claims about 300 affiliates as its own and its growth in the last three years has been phenomenal. The show is an interesting forum covering topics that many people either are afraid to talk about or simply do not have the opportunity to explore. I am not afraid of these topics; I am energized and challenged by them.

The Format

On *Dreamland*, every week I have a guest, whether it is someone from the world of science or a past life expert or even someone who specializes in alien abductions. My guests are either spectacular or they crash in flames. When you do a live show week after week, it is a throw of the dice. I let my guests tell their story. I don't interrupt them and demand proof for every statement they make; I am not a contentious interviewer. It's like inviting a guest into your home and then getting into a huge argument with them. I don't think that is good radio.

There are rare occasions on which I have been provoked into an argument because someone has come after me and I come right back at them, but I don't like having to do that because it is rarely an intelligent discourse. I would rather let my audience judge whether it sounds real and credible or phony and laughable. The guest will inevitably either dig their own grave or climb their own mountain as it were. In contrast to Coast to Coast, which I can carry for five hours, it is important for me to have the specific input of someone who has expertise in a particular field relating to *Dreamland* issues.

The Topics

Dreamland covers two main topics and occasionally I'll deviate from those. The topics I cover on *Dreamland* are things that I have addressed as long as I have been in talk radio. In short, *Dreamland* is an official extension of my own interest in the topics of life after death, the paranormal, mental telepathy, and various spiritually related topics, as well as my interest in learning about whether or not there is intelligent, extra-terrestrial life. The show features discussions on all·these topics and even on the entire, controversial unidentified flying object phenomenon, including UFO sightings, the accounts of aliens, the accounts of abductions of people by aliens, etc.

One of my most regular guests, Linda Moulton Howe is an illustration of what I mean by being open to finding the truth. She contributes to *Dreamland* with her weekly updates of the latest news in such topics as the environment, emerging diseases, UFO sightings and non-human encounters and other various paranormal activities. Linda is the top in her field for investigating such unexplained phenomena and has gone in directions that quite honestly others have been afraid to. Her books and documentaries provide us with the evidence to begin to piece together what might be happening in the world around us and beyond.

When you look into the sky and see all the stars and the planets which exist in the universe, it seems to me that you would be naive to dismiss the possibility of the existence of intelligent life somewhere out there in the universe. Have intelligent life forms visited our planet? Do these life forms visit us? Are these life forms actually here among us? I really don't have a conclusive answer to any of this. But I am open to learning about these things. Now, I personally have had a couple of strange experiences which have certainly compelled me to do this radio program in the first place, and which compel me to continue this show as long as I can.

My Precognition Experience

One experience that is relevant to *Dreamland* involves my first (and only, so far) 'precognition experience.' This was many years ago, while I was still in rock radio, and I was living in Santa Barbara, California. I was sitting in my apartment at the time and watching the evening news. Suddenly, I had this strong feeling wash over me that someone was going to hit my car. It was a bizarre sensation as I felt wave after wave after wave of this feeling that my car would be hit. I could not ignore this feeling. As the feeling grew in intensity, I finally got up to look out the window to see my car. My car was parked on the street in front of my apartment. Nothing seemed out of the ordinary, so I just returned to watch the news.

This feeling resumed and it would not go away. It was as though a voice were repeatedly telling me, "Someone is about to hit your car, someone is about to hit your car, someone is about to hit your car...." I was beginning to get impatient with myself and even somewhat irritated. Eventually, the feeling got so strong again, I got up to look out the window at my car. The car was fine. I then noticed a man walking down the sidewalk. As I watched, this man walked up to his car, which was parked directly in front of my car. He unlocked his car, got in, started his engine, put the car into reverse, and hit my car. I couldn't believe it.

This scared me so much that I started to shake and actually fell to my knees, a tingling sensation going down my spine. Obviously, I had had a case of precognition. I recovered quickly enough to open the sliding glass window I had been looking through, and shouted at the man that I had seen him hit my car. He immediately stopped and said, "Okay, okay, I'm stopping." I then went out to him, much more calmly, and we exchanged information for insurance purposes. My car did not sustain much damage, but I would never forget this strange experience of knowing with absolute certainty that my car was going to be hit and it was. Where this came from I have no idea. Was it something from my mind, some past ability that is just now being developed, or was it an angel, or was it something else? I don't know.

My UFO Sightings

I have seen many unusual things in the desert. In fact, I see so much that I can't—and don't want to—tell every single flash of light or weird thing I witness. But I have had what I would call two 'major' sightings recently that illustrate how strange experiences have influenced my view on the topics covered in *Dreamland*.

The first occurred while I was still working at KDWN and making my regular commute between Pahrump and Las Vegas. At the time, my wife, Ramona was also working at KDWN and she usually commuted with me. Anyway, we were on our way back to Pahrump, and it was about 11:25pm. I was about a mile away from my home at that time. My wife was in the passenger seat and for some reason she abruptly turned around.

"What the hell is that?!" She said.

"I don't know," I said, not having seen anything myself at that point.

"Stop the car," she demanded.

So I immediately pulled over to the side of the road. It was in the summer and although it was late at night it was blood warm, in the upper 90s. It was also dead quiet; you could hear a cricket at quarter of a mile. I turned off the engine and got out of the car. Then I turned around, looked down the road and saw a sight that actually stood the hair up on the back of my neck. Hovering over the road and coming up behind us was a giant, triangular craft, about 150 feet from one point of the triangle to another. It had a strobing red light on the front part of the triangle and it had two bright, white lights at each point of the triangle. I also believe the craft was above the ground about 150 feet.

In a short while, this bizarre craft came directly over our car. The craft did not fly; it floated. Flying requires aerodynamic support. In other words, a craft has to be going fast enough for air to traverse the wings and support the craft. This thing could not have been going more than 20 miles per hour. And other than perhaps a hang glider, there is nothing that can do that. This thing was operating in apparent defiance of gravity. There was no way of knowing what was moving this craft because it was silent. Dead silent. It did not appear to have an engine.

Ramona and I stood gazing at this craft until it floated out across Pahrump Valley and disappeared. What did I see? I don't know. I would call this a UFO experience or a close encounter of probably the second kind. I didn't actually meet any aliens or see any or communicate with anything in the craft.

The other really big sighting I had was a daylight event. Ramona and I were walking up the driveway of our home on Memorial Day and we saw a big silver disk, following in the contrail of a military jet. We had enough time to rush inside and get the binoculars and see it stop for a moment, then disappear to the south.

So, there you have it. My three strange experiences, one which I call a precognition experience and two that I will call my UFO experiences. I did not make any of this up. I experienced these things, and that is that. And it really doesn't matter that much to me if anyone believes me. But I assure you I pay close attention when other people relate their experiences with me. I will continue to make the topics of the paranormal, afterlife experiences, mental telepathy, UFOs and the like the focus of *Dreamland*. I feel that I must.

Alien Sightings and Visitations

I do not believe thousands of people all around the world have just imagined things or made up reports about experiences that relate to these topics. I don't believe, for example, that some of the UFO sightings many people have seen are not real. Thousands of people seeing the same thing cannot *all* be wrong. I know my experiences were not things I imagined; they were real. Granted, there are probably sightings that can be explained as natural phenomena, but many others cannot.

I believe that we have been visited by beings from outside of our world. Although I am quite skeptical that anyone has actually been abducted by such beings (although I continue to air reports of supposed abductions), of course, I don't know for sure. I suppose no one can know for sure until such beings land on the White House lawn. Nonetheless, I also believe that our government probably knows about such visits, but does not want to reveal the details lest this induce utter panic in the American populous. I think people really would go into a panic should such a visitation occur and become widely known, especially if such a thing is publicized through the national media as a grand announcement from the White House. I believe it would completely upset the social and religious structure of our country. There might even be anarchy. But I also believe the people should be given the truth. The outcome of such information brought public has been an ongoing debate in the UFO community.

I have been openly discussing these things on the radio long enough to know that people who are very religious would most likely believe that visitors from out of this world are devils. And the first little green or gray guy walking down the plank of a flying saucer would be so filled with lead that it would be all over in no time. That is, all over for us because if there was a whole fleet out there, they would probably blow us away in retaliation. There are many people who actually pray for such open contact, as though this may result in our salvation. It seems to me that if aliens had any brains at all they would not make themselves apparent to us. And if there are any aliens reading this book, take my advice, don't make contact with us yet. We're not ready for you.

Am I being cynical by thinking that our government keeps things from us? I don't think so. Consider some of the things our government *is* known to have kept from Americans. Would anyone have believed that the government would have deliberately fed children radiation, just to see what effect radiation might have on them? No, of course not. But Hazel O'Leary, the US Secretary of Energy, recently admitted that our government did do such experiments on children. This is only one of a number of really horrible things that our government has done. Would our government tell us? No.

Several years ago when a very rare, incurable, fast-acting, highly contagious Ebola virus broke out in Reston, Virginia, did the government inform us about that? They did not. Suppose there was a comet like Hale-Bopp that was heading for earth, and it was expected to bring the cataclysmic destruction of many of earth's inhabitants. Would our government tell us? Probably not. Nor would our government tell us if beings from somewhere in the universe came to visit.

As far as the importance of Roswell and Area 51, there's so much evidence that *something* has happened and continues to happen daily. The Air Force has gone out of its way to explain it away and have in fact done the exact opposite; I think they may have even made believers out of skeptics in many cases. Take the fact that Congressman Schiff pursued investigations and only then was it "mysteriously" discovered that crucial records were missing. That's no coincidence. But I believe the American people know better than that; they know instinctively when they are being lied to. The importance in these events lies in the basic fact of their existence, of unexplained phenomena occurring all around us. We may not know what it is, but we do know *something* is happening.

Ghosts & the Afterlife

As for the possibility of an afterlife, this subject matter fascinates me like no other. I believe we have a soul. True, no one has ever come back from death and given us a report on their experience. But I am really a hands-on sort of person and I will continue to look for evidence that tells me what will happen after this life. The best photograph I have ever received came from a man in Arizona. The stone mason who had done some remodeling work in the basement of an old house took the photo to include in his portfolio.

In looking at the photo, you'll discern what appears to be the white, cloudy outline of some being hovering in the room where this stone mason had done his work. I believe this being was a ghost. I happen to believe ghosts are spirit beings (probably spirits of the dead) which are trapped here for some reason on earth.

Apparently, there were at least two work crews on the house who just walked off the job. Eventually, this particular stone mason did the work. Yet, during the course of the work, the workers did have some unusual experiences. On one occasion, a couple of workers were going up a stairway, when all of a sudden a strong invisible force pushed them back. They toppled backward down the stairs as a result. Clearly, there was something in that house. Again, I think it was a spirit, a ghost.

The Unexplained

There have been many, many accounts of people who for all intents and purposes had died. They were no longer breathing, their heart stopped, and so on. And yet they would come back to life after a period, maybe a few minutes, or an hour, or whatever. In each case, they reported very similar experiences. They all seem to report going through a tunnel with a bright white light at the end, followed by the meeting of relatives who had passed away, the fast-forward film of events of their lives from youth on, and so on. For me, this provides a certain amount of encouragement that when you die, there is another place that you go. How do we prove it? I don't know.

Near Death Experiences

I love to get experts on *Dreamland* to talk about these things. I get doctors and scientists as well as people who actually had these experiences. For instance, Dannion Brinkley is one person I like to have on to talk about his life and death experiences. Not only has he had a near death experience where he encountered non-human beings, but he also acquired the skill of prophecy. Even now he possesses the ability to read minds and has dedicated his life to bettering the lives of the sick and elderly. His story is utterly fascinating to me because it presents the possibilities and you can hardly argue with his accuracy and his abilities, given to him by these strange beings. Here is more tangible proof than anyone has seen before.

Open for Interpretation

Strange Universe described me as a "prophet of the paranormal, a Moses of sorts." I feel what I am doing is significant not so much in the sense that I 'convert' people, because I don't, but rather, that people are provided a forum in which they can discuss issues of importance not as readily accepted in other mediums. I make the assumption that, all things being equal, my listeners are adults, capable of making the distinction between fraud and fact. I simply make the presentation; they make the decision to believe or disbelieve.

So, why not have an open forum such as *Dreamland?* After all, if we were to discover that there is intelligent life out there, it would be the story of this century. If there is proof that there is life after death, this would solve one of the great mysteries which mankind has always had. People need *Dreamland* and people want *Dreamland.* The topics of discussion are controversial, but they are important. *Dreamland* will continue to entertain and inform, going where others fear to tread.

10

THE FUTURE

I just want to say a few things about the future here: America's and my own.

As for myself, I have seen more success with my radio programs *Coast to Coast AM* and *Dreamland* in the past three years than at any other time. Both shows have experienced spectacular growth and I am very thankful. Obviously, it is my professional hope that my success will continue. I am not and will not be plagued by the greed for growth. Quite frankly, whatever the future holds for me on a professional level, I will be forever thankful for the opportunities I have had, interacting with people the way I do, and for the information and enjoyment I have brought millions of people. I truly enjoy this job immensely. No, better yet, I love my job.

I think of Ted Turner who once said, "Success is like an empty bag." In other words, success in and of itself is not enough. And money is certainly not the goal. The most important thing is doing something that I love and developing my talent to do it. I wish to drive myself for the purpose of improving my craft.

From a personal standpoint, I hope to continue to be with the woman who I love so much. And I wish to do so in the atmosphere that I love so much. This means my hopes for the future do not include moving into a mansion somewhere. I very much feel comfortable and happy in the home I now occupy, modest though it may be. I wish very much to continue living the lifestyle I now live. It is simple, quiet, and makes life enjoyable.

America's Future

I guess I view my personal future quite favorably. But the future of America is a whole different story. When I think of America's future, I somehow think it more appropriate to ponder in what way I should pray for America. I have reflected on the state of America's soul, the broad view of things in this country from the perspective of the Quickening, and all the other concerns I have voiced about this country and its current unfortunate condition. I think we are past the point of no return, and I think America is going to become something else. And that something will not be altogether as good and promising as it once was.

It is difficult for me to write about my hopes for the future of America. The reason it is so difficult for me is that my hopes for this country are not many. I do not see a good future for America, at least the way it is headed right now. Things are not going well in this country. Most Americans are in denial about a lot of things. Most of us have our heads in the sand, economically, politically, and socially. We are experiencing a rapid deterioration in each one of these areas.

I know this sounds black and dreary; I don't like being negative. I would like to paint a rosy, idyllic picture of humanity's future. In my prayers, there *is* a good picture for the outcome of America, at the very least. You would have to separate my hopes for this country from my prayers. My hopes for America are virtually non-existent. My prayers are very much for the return of earlier values, the glue that made America a great country in the first place. America, I pray, would be great again. America, I pray, would be the leader of the world. But when I open my eyes and I see the reality of the way things are, I just can't lie. I can't tell you that I think things are going to turn out well because I just don't think it is possible with the current path our country has taken.

223

I would say that the future of the world to a large extent is determined on an individual basis. We all have choices to make about the way the world is going and the best thing we can do is to keep our eyes and minds open to what is going on around us. As I said before, we need to treat each other better, with more respect. It is my hope that things will improve, so that our children's future would not be so bleak. In fact I have dedicated my book, *The Quickening* to my son and to all the children of future generations. I just hope people get the message.

Is There Still Hope?

I have often been asked, since I have my finger on the metaphorical pulse of America, whether I still think there is hope for the world. I would say that I do think so. Of course, while man can take responsibility for some things, certain parts of the world are beyond repair and we will realistically not be able to change them. I am not suggesting that humans live in constant fear and paranoia of what will happen next, far from it. What I *do* suggest is that we look farther ahead than just a few days, to the future we are creating *today* for ourselves. Without a miracle (and I don't rule out miracles), we are headed for whatever is next, probably to change, to become something else. On the way to that 'becoming,' being informed about different aspects of the world's situation and accepting that the reality of our world is not necessarily a bright one are some of the first steps in determining whether tomorrow's world will be a better place.

SOME WORDS OF APPRECIATION

Life can be an amazing experience. It amazes me at times when I reflect on my life and compare my rather inauspicious beginning to the way my life is now. I started by growing up in a turbulent household. I did not like nor did I do particularly well in school. I did not have a chance to cultivate any friendships because my family moved around so much. I was almost always in trouble, at school, at home, everywhere. And there was every indication that I would either end up dead or in jail.

I believe it was my fate that I would discover radio and that I would discover an innate interest and a talent for radio. As I consider how my life has unfolded over the years, I can see how everything seemed meant to be. And after all I have gone through, even the many years of barely subsisting, and the many years of moving from one end of the country to the other, I can see how it has all come together. I now know I have been specially blessed as I not only became a very good broadcaster, but also have been fortunate enough to excel to a level rarely experienced by most people in this business.

My success has been the result of being the right person, at the right place at the right time. I have recognized opportunity and I followed through. The last few years have proven to be very good years for the talk radio business. The popularity of talk radio has grown tremendously. When Larry King ended his night talk radio career, this was an important opportunity and a significant turning point in my own career. Also there have been many people who have helped me along the way, and I am grateful to all of them. I am grateful to my mother who encouraged me when I discovered Ham radio. I am grateful to the general at Amarillo Air Force Base who made it possible for me to experience commercial radio broadcasting for the first time. I am grateful to the Air Force for introducing me to the orient, which resulted in my incredible radio experience in Okinawa. I am grateful to all the radio stations (the small ones, the large ones, and all those in between) which helped me learn my craft. I am grateful to Claire Reese at KDWN in Las Vegas, who gave me my first break in talk radio. I am grateful to Alan Corbeth for making it possible for my show to be syndicated all over America and beyond.

I am grateful to my wife, Ramona, who has encouraged me and helped me to succeed. Without her I could not have done what I have done to this day. And I am immensely grateful to my many, many listeners. I am grateful to my long time listeners and to my new listeners as my show continues to grow. I am a fortunate man and am grateful for all I have. Life is good.

Index

The Art of Talk
audiobook, 4 cassettes, 4 hrs. 30 min.

Performed by Art Bell in his studio and based on his book. Also includes audio clips from his early days in radio. This recording is destined to become an audio classic!!   *$23.95*

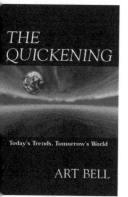

The Quickening: Today's Trends, Tomorrow's World
paperback, 336 pages

The Quickening calls attention to the acceleration of every aspect of human existence as we head toward the 21st century. Art Bell astutely examines the underlying forces of today's trends and offers thoughts on coming to terms with these trends.   *$15.95*

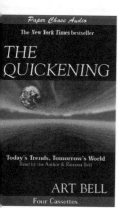

The Quickening: Today's Trends, Tomorrow's World
audiobook, 4 cassettes, 6hrs.

Performed by Art Bell and Ramona Bell in his studio and based on his book.   *$24.95*

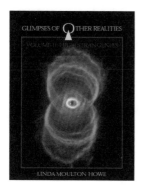